ONCE UPON A RUSSIA

VOICES FROM A VANISHED ERA

Foreword by
SIR RODERIC LYNE

Edited by
STEVEN A. FISHER

Forest Cat
PRESS

Once Upon a Russia: Voices From a Vanished Era
Copyright @2025 Steven A. Fisher

All rights reserved. No part of this book may be used or reproduced in any manner whatsoever without written permission.

Copyright for each individual essay and photograph (unless otherwise indicated in the Photo Credits) included in this anthology remains with the respective contributor. All works appear with the express permission of their creators. No part of any essay or photograph may be reproduced, reprinted, or otherwise used without the explicit consent of the author or rights holder.

For information, address KGL Ventures LLC, 127 West Oak Street, Chicago, IL 60610

To contact Steven A. Fisher:
stevenfisherciti.com

Library of Congress Control Number: 2025946679

Publisher's Cataloging-in-Publication Data:

Names: Fisher, Steven A., editor.
Title: Once upon a Russia : voices from a vanished era / Steven A. Fisher, Editor.
Description: Chicago, IL: Forest Cat Press, 2025.
Identifiers: LCCN: 2025946679 | ISBN: 978-1-7377663-3-9 (hardcover) | 978-1-7377663-4-6 (paperback) | 978-1-7377663-5-3 (ebook)
Subjects: LCSH: Soviet Union--History--20th century. | Soviet Union--Civilization--20th century. | Russia (Federation)--History--20th century. | Russia (Federation)--Civilization--20th century. | Russia (Federation)--History--21st century. | Russia (Federation)--Civilization--21st century. | Essays. | BISAC HISTORY / Russia / Soviet Era | HISTORY / Russia / Post-Soviet | POLITICAL SCIENCE / World / Russian & Soviet

Classification: LCC: DK510.76 O63 F57 2025 | DDC: 947.086--dc23

Printed in the United States of America

In Russia's Shadowed Silence

CONTENTS

Foreword, Sir Roderic Lyne 9
Introduction, By the Editor 13

I MISSION

A Moment of Fate, Richard Sobel 16
One Week in August, Bob Foresman 18
"You Know Nothing About America!", Ambassador (Ret.) John Beyrle 20
We Wanted the Best, Alan Bigman 22
Beyond the Pipeline, John Dabbar 24
Building a Legal Bridge, Doran Doeh 26
Gorbi Mania!, Hans Wicks 28
Dreams of Saratov, Thomas Fallows 30
And There Was Light, Brook Horowitz 32
Moscow's Finest, Brian Lee 34
Utopia, Ambassador (Ret.) Michael Tay 36
Expats and the Russia Balance Sheet, Andrew C. Kuchins 38

II CHANGE

The Journey that Mattered, Steven Fisher 42
Warm West to Frigid East, Bryan Dougall 44
Russia's "Années Folles", Hadrien Fraissinet 46
The Metro Tour, Brian Zimbler 48
Street Smart, Kira Gruger 50
So Many Windows, Rachel Polonsky 52
Kaif, Michael Pugh 54
Crossing Tverskaya, Michael Tappan 56
The Found One, Jennifer Neufeld 58
Kitchen Table Wisdom, Daniel Satinsky 60
No More Bread Lines, Meena Mylvaganam 62
Going Bananas, Robert Stephenson 64

My First Job, John Stavis 66
Mastering the Art of Cooking in Moscow, Jennifer Eremeeva.......... 68
A Capital Perspective, Guy Archer 70
Our Home in Moscow, Jim Balaschak 72
Our Russian Daughter, Bhaskar Katta 74
Lasting Friendships, Connie Barcenas 76
Miles to Go before We Sleep…, John Sartorius.................................. 78
Across Frontiers, Jeffrey Mankoff 80
Shifting Plates, Solid Cores, Hans Grisel.. 82
Legal Reckoning, William Pomeranz 84
Crime and Punishment, Jamison Firestone 86
Sergei, William Benton Whisenhunt 88
The Coup, David Cant 90
No Rebound in Moscow, Bernard Sucher 92
One Too Many Blessings, Nora FitzGerald 94
Just the Essentials, David Jenkins... 96
The Gray Men Are Gone, Jeffrey R. Costello...................................... 98
Full Circle, Alex Geller 100
Unlearning Russia, Stephen O'Connor 102
Notes From Novodevichy, Karl Stoltz 104
Tver, Russia, 2007, Jason Gresh 106
No Crime, No Punishment, Eloisa Klecheski 108
The Corner Stop-n-Shop, Elizabeth Sullivan.................................... 110

III EVENTS

Right Place, Right Time: A Life Saved in Moscow, Robert Courtney .. 114
Russia's Long Road to Tomorrow, Ben Aris...................................... 116
Cowboy Law at its Finest, John Hewko 118
Turkey in Moscow, Richard Conn 120
The Candidate and the Bet, William Shor 122
Vodka with Attitude, Stephen T. Cruty... 124
A Tale of Crisis, Currency, and Couture, Peter Westin 126
Lost in Transition, Dominique Menu 128

Russia and the European Approach, Seppo Remes 130
Saturday with the Governor, Eugene Belin 132
Moscow Memories, Steve Ridlington 134
For the Love of Izmailovo, Constance McCaslin............................. 136
Riding Russian Railways, Scott Gehlbach 138
Stitches, Brian D. Taylor.. 140
Romanovs, Bolsheviks, Communists, Patricia E. Dowden............. 142

IV ABSURDITY

1996, Grozny, Republic of Chechnya, Russia, T. Hawk Sunshine . 146
TIR, Laura Brank... 148
The Art of Motion, Steven Thunem 150
Niva Queen for a Day, Michele A. Berdy... 152
The Taxi "Chek", Alexander Waechter... 154
Swift, Unforgiving, and Paid for in Full, Douglas Steele................ 156
Siberian Ledger, Richard Creitzman 158
Silver Streak Redemption, Charles Borden 160
The Most Memorable Look & See Trip, Corrado Giaquinto.......... 162
Welcome to the U.S.S.R.: The Sony Story, Paul Melling................. 164
A Mixed Reception, Richard Dean.. 166
One Day in August, Ambassador (Ret.) Eric S. Rubin 168
Vladivostok: Briefings, Beatings, and Borderlines, Adam A. Blanco ... 170
Halloween, Eric Luhmann... 172
Chelnokism, Joshua B. Tulgan 174
Invisible Borders, Mikki Mahan 176
"When Your Son Looks Like Your Neighbor", Thomas Firestone.. 178
Garderob, Marc Polonsky 180
Moscow Nights, Paul Ostling 182
Unreliable Memories, Alistair Stobie.. 184
Stranger in a Strange Land, Peter Enright.. 186
The Excremental Vision, Dan Goldberg.. 188
Sic Transit Gloria Mundi, Steven Solnick 190
Forgotten at the Gate, Ilkka Salonen.. 192

V HUMILITY

Russia for Me, Jonathan C. Knaus 196
The Banya Drives Any Ailment from the Body,   Ambassador (Ret.) Allan Mustard 198
The Blue Light of Russian Souls, Marie de La Ville Baugé 200
Endless Shades of Green, Sarah Waybright Barr 202
Foreigners, Far and Near, Catherine Breen 204
The Better Part of Valor, Matthew Roazen 206
The Movers, Stuart Lawson 208

VI DESOLATION

Four Hundred Cows, No Fish, Anders Åslund 212
Siberian Oil, Kevin McKinney 214
The Risk of Success, Matthew Murray 216
Komi Story, Jan Dauman 218
The Rules Unwritten, Topper Power 220
Of Cold Vodka and Hot Banyas, Steven Parker 222
A Partner and a Cat, Ivan Scalfarotto 224
Concrete Dream, Ambassador (Ret.) Michael Klecheski 226
No Happy Ending, Edward Verona 228
Born in Occupation, Living in Freedom, Merle Pormeister 230
The Murder of Boris Nemtsov, Ambassador (Ret.) John Tefft 232
The Memory That Stayed, John McNaughton 234

Acknowledgments 237
Photo Credits 239
About the Editor 243

FOREWORD
Sir Roderic Lyne

In *Once Upon a Russia* Steven Fisher has assembled more than one hundred vignettes that brilliantly illustrate the mixed emotions of Westerners who lived and worked in Russia through an era of rapid, unpredictable, and ultimately tragic transition.

For almost twenty years, from the late 1980s to the end of Putin's first term as president, the USSR and then Russia was converging with and opening up to the West. By the turn of the millennium, in the words of Edward Verona, "Russia was unmistakably moving toward a market economy and a freer society." Three successive leaders—Gorbachev, Yeltsin, and Putin—pursued a strategy of integration. Putin took this to its zenith, building ever-closer relationships with the EU, NATO, and Western leaders. In July 2002, he achieved the ultimate accolade of full membership in the G8, with the right to host a future summit (held in St. Petersburg in 2006).

For the past two decades, since Putin abandoned economic reform in favor of grand larceny and turned against the West following his humiliation with the grotesquely mishandled Beslan massacre and then the Orange Revolution in Ukraine, the pendulum has swung ever more sharply in the opposite direction.

In Putin's first term, relations with the West were friendlier, more transparent, and more cooperative than at any time in Russia's history. We worked together across all eleven time zones in almost every sector. Western governments were even helping Russia to dismantle nuclear submarines, destroy chemical weapons, and retrain soldiers for civilian life.

Now, eleven years since Putin began to wage war on Ukraine, and three and a half years since his full-scale invasion, the hostility between Russia and the West equals or exceeds the most acute tensions of the Cold War. As William Pomeranz concludes, "Instead of integration, we are once again stuck with a new East-West divide that will take years to overcome."

Ben Aris labels Russia "famously a country of extremes ... nothing is easy. Yet you feel intensely alive there." "Before relations with the West frayed," writes Eugene Belin, "it was a land of dynamism, risk, and reward." To Eric Luhmann, Moscow was "crackling with opportunity, corruption, and more than a little mystery," and to Topper Power, "a place of vast possibilities and profound risk."

The witnesses in this book echo the centuries-old struggle to understand Russia by those of us who are drawn to the country and its people. In Catherine the Great's reign, Sir George Macartney spent two years in Russia and wrote of "a nation of inconsistence, contradiction and paradox, uniting in themselves the most opposite extremes; hating the stranger, they copy him; affecting originality, they are the slaves of imitation; magnificent and slovenly; irreligious yet superstitious; at once proud and abject, rapacious and prodigal."[1]

By chance, I spent the summer of 1961 in Russia. This drew me into the fascination of trying to comprehend a place that was (for the most part) geographically, historically, ethnically, and culturally part of Europe—and yet far apart from it. So it remains. Since then, I have totted up eleven years of my life in Russia, spread over six decades, constantly in search of enlightenment. For me Russia is a place where you can dig forever and never reach the bottom. As Jennifer Neufeld eloquently puts it, "The great Russian soul was too vast for me ever to understand."

There is a side to Russia, reflected throughout Steven Fisher's book, known to those who have lived there: friendship with ordinary people. Putin's Russia, like the pre-Gorbachev Soviet Union, is ruled by a regime that is threatening, cruel, and massively corrupt, but that does not describe the totality of the Russian people. Russians have been the victims of Putin's regime. It has inflicted a devastating war on them, taken away their freedom, stolen their wealth, run down their public services, and, humiliatingly, placed Russia in hock to China and North Korea. Those in power, as described by Jamison Firestone, "took what they wanted and the price was paid by those trying to build something better and the people they were trying to help."

---

[1] Sir George Macartney, *An Account of Russia*, London, 1768.

From the late 1980s it became possible for Westerners to experience normal human relations with Russians, hitherto interdicted by the KGB. The book testifies to "lasting friendships founded on respect and trust," wrote Richard Sobel; to "human talent," observed Bryan Dougall; to "friendships that endure," in the words of Connie Barcenas; and to "brilliant, diligent and warm-hearted Russian colleagues," recalled Eugene Belin. That has been my experience, too.

Thomas Fallows encapsulates the dichotomy between the people and the regime: "My love for the Russian people is profound. Their generosity, humor, and resilience have left an indelible mark on me. And yet I am often struck by the cruelty of the system that has governed their lives—whether in the oppressive past or in its grim resurgence today."

It will take years for Russia to recover from the consequences of Putin's war and his regime's criminal mismanagement. We cannot tell what lies beyond that but must hope that some of the seeds sown more than twenty years ago will germinate. For now, for me, and I imagine for most of this book's authors, John McKnaughton's parting words say it all:

"Russia gave me so much. But now, it also gives me grief. And that grief clouds even the brightest memories."

Sir Roderic Lyne served as a British diplomat in the USSR and Russian Federation from 1972–74, 1987–90, and 2000–2004. In 1991, he was the last head of the Soviet Department in the Foreign Office. Since 2005, he has visited Russia fifty-eight times in various capacities.

INTRODUCTION
By the Editor

It is a curious thing to look back on a life once spent in Russia—a place where strong impressions and unusual experiences have since blended into a complex mixture of achievement and disappointment, fascination and frustration, clarity and contradiction. Some memories remain distinct and sharp; others have faded, becoming harder to place, yet no less meaningful.

I am the editor of this collection, a compiler of personal histories shaped by time spent in Russia. I offer this volume not as an outside observer but as someone who took part in the story—at least in parts. Like the contributors whose reflections fill these pages, I experienced something of the unpredictable rhythm of Russian life and, for a time, found myself shaped by it.

What I saw, what I did, what I overheard—whether over crystal flutes in velvet-draped, storied restaurants or chipped teacups at crowded kitchen tables, whether stiffly voiced in official meetings or quietly shared in stairwells—none of it, I think, will be repeated in quite the same way. Russia, after all, is like a long, unfolding novel—complex in its narrative and still in the process of being written.

For those of us who were part of it—whether for a lifetime or a lark—it left its marks. You may have left Russia, but it is not so quick to leave you. It lodges in the back of your mind like a line from Fyodor Dostoyevsky that you can't quite understand. It survives in coat pockets as old Metro tokens and faded receipts from long-closed cafés. It returns in dreams as snow beneath streetlights and the faint smell of boiled buckwheat.

Once Upon a Russia: Voices From a Vanished Era, was shaped by the recognition that the Russia we experienced no longer exists in the same form. The decision to bring these stories together—to preserve and contemplate them—felt both timely and necessary. I hoped to create not a definitive portrait, but a chorus of voices—each distinct, forming a tapestry of a memory that captures a Russia now receding into history.

I sent out the call, and the responses arrived—more varied, vivid, and numerous than I could have imagined. Over one hundred writers (all non-Russian) answered, each offering little gems: a fragment of experience, a sliver of Russia refracted through the prism of memory and time.

Some found their way to Russia by chance, through marriage or the pull of circumstance. Others arrived as bankers, lawyers, engineers, journalists, scholars, diplomats, artists, or idealists. A few planned to stay only months but remained for decades. Some left with wealth; others departed with only a suitcase and never looked back.

Yet every contributor to this volume was willing to sift through their recollections, revisit half-forgotten scenes, and share them here—sometimes with affection, sometimes with ache, and often with the wry, precise irony that has long been essential to experiencing life in Russia.

These tales do not pretend to explain Russia—something many Russians themselves might call impossible. Instead, they offer accounts of the absurd, glimpses of streets transformed, portraits of unexpected relationships, conversations with officials veering from comic to somber, and insights into both achievement and tragedy that have marked the country's recent history. Some are sharp and direct; others quieter. What unites them is not a singular theme or style but a shared sense of lived experience. For those who once knew this country, these stories may feel like the return of familiar voices not heard in years. For those who never visited, they may offer a glimpse into a time and place that can no longer be experienced.

This book is, in part, a record—a way to preserve what might otherwise fade. It may also be read as a collection of personal notes: thoughtful, sometimes affectionate, occasionally blunt. Above all, it is a gathering of perspectives that together offer a glimpse of a particular time in Russia's long and complex story.

Welcome to *Once Upon a Russia: Voices From a Vanished Era*. You are in thoughtful company.

I
MISSION

I was ready to throw myself into any abyss,
as long as something new and unpredictable awaited me at the bottom.

Я готов был броситься в любую бездну,
лишь бы на дне её ожидало меня нечто
новое, непредсказуемое.

Mikhail Lermontov, A Hero of Our Time
Михаил Лермонтов, Герой нашего времени
1840

A MOMENT OF FATE
Richard Sobel

My professional journey in Russia began in early 1991, when I moved to Moscow to work for Batterymarch Financial Management on the Soviet Companies Fund, a groundbreaking initiative co-sponsored by the Soviet government to invest in joint ventures with foreign partners. We were graciously housed in a grand residence in Lenin Hills and escorted through leading military-industrial enterprises, often in formerly closed cities, to evaluate commercial projects.

That August, our investor tour was overtaken by the Soviet coup d'état attempt. History shifted beneath our feet, and for several unforgettable days we found ourselves inside the belly of the bear. I still see the long line of Soviet tanks rolling past our office, the tense dinner at our residence where Russian and Soviet military men confronted one another, and the surreal moment when we stood on a tank that had switched sides to support the protesters. As the coup unraveled, we celebrated with friends in Kiev and Leningrad, feeling we had witnessed the turning of an era.

Though uncertain of our safety and prepared to flee, we chose to stay. It was a moment of fate. Yeltsin, Sobchak, and many others—including people we knew well—stood with courage and clarity, rejecting the weight of communism and autocracy. As the Soviet Union crumbled and fifteen republics claimed independence, we felt a powerful sense of hope rising from the ruins.

Batterymarch's initiative was early, and as the collapse accelerated, I moved to the European Bank for Reconstruction and Development (EBRD) in Moscow. Beginning in 1994, I helped build two private equity platforms: Baring Vostok and Alfa Capital Partners. Together we invested in companies like VimpelCom, Borjomi, World Class, and Burren Energy. Those years were a remarkable time. We worked side by side with entrepreneurs, advisors, and foreign investors, believing deeply in the vast potential of a new market economy.

What stayed with me most was Russia's extraordinary human capital—its resilience, intelligence, and determination to master international finance, strategy, and management. We built profitable businesses and lasting friendships founded on respect and trust.

In recent years, I have watched with deep sadness as the old guard reclaimed power, smothering reform, silencing enterprise, and steering the country back toward control and imperial ambition.

Yet I carry this enduring belief: when conditions allow and leaders inspire, human potential is boundless. I still hope to see that promise return to Russia within my lifetime.

Richard Sobel is an American pioneer in Russian private equity. In 1991, he was with a U.S. investment firm during the coup and later joined the EBRD. He then founded and led Baring Vostok and Alfa Capital Partners. Over his career, he launched five private equity funds in Russia, raised $900 million, achieved four IPOs, served on two public boards and various portfolio and partnership boards, and held roles on the American Chamber of Commerce board and as a trustee of the European University at Saint Petersburg.

ONE WEEK IN AUGUST
Bob Foresman

"Want to go to Kiev this weekend?" Dima asked. "They've got great local beer." It was July 1991. I was interning at CBS News in Moscow, living with a Russian family in a communal apartment near Lubyanka Square and mangling Soviet newscast summaries for American audiences. I liked to think I was warming U.S.–Soviet relations, one mistranslation at a time.

I'd met Dima two years earlier while studying at the Moscow Energy Institute. We American students learned Russian through flat beer, cheap champagne, and bad vodka with our new friends.

Kiev, as it was still called then, was charming and seemed more relaxed than Moscow. While wandering down St. Andrew's Descent, we stopped in a flower shop called Roksolana. Behind the counter stood an indescribably radiant young woman arranging flowers. I stared too long, then said to my friends, "Эта девушка будет моей женой" (*Eta devushka budet moyey zhenoy*). That girl will be my wife. She wasn't interested. But I came back in mid-August and finally convinced her to go on a date. We made plans for the next day—her birthday, August 18.

On August 19, I woke to news of a coup. Gorbachev had been arrested, and in Kiev the rumors were that he'd been killed. I ran to the flower shop. Luda helped me find a train back to Moscow. Technically, I wasn't allowed to leave Moscow without permission under my visa, and I risked detention in Kiev. More troubling, I feared Luda could be at risk for being with an American.

Back in Moscow, I joined the crowds at the barricades around Yeltsin's resistance effort. By the following morning, the coup had collapsed. Fear gave way to euphoria. It felt like witnessing Boston in 1776 or Paris in 1789.

I was supposed to start graduate school at Harvard in Soviet studies the next week. For a moment, I considered staying. But after talking with my parents and the program director, I sobered up and went. I was spontaneous—but not reckless.

In a single week, I fell in love and watched an empire unravel.

Now, thirty-four years, one marriage, and five kids later, Luda and I are trying to process the Russia–Ukraine war. The faith that carried us across borders, through fear and doubt and five kids, still holds. Bent, maybe. But not broken.

Now, we watch and pray—for peace between the two countries that brought us together.

Bob Foresman spent five years in Ukraine in the 1990s, including leading the International Finance Corporation's Small-Scale Privatization Project, and fifteen years in Moscow, where he served as regional CEO of Dresdner Kleinwort Wasserstein, deputy chairman of Renaissance Capital, and country head for Barclays Group. He was vice chairman of UBS Investment Bank, based in New York, until 2020, and he remains active in finance and advisory work both internationally and in the United States.

"YOU KNOW NOTHING ABOUT AMERICA!"
Ambassador (Ret.) John Beyrle

In 1977, at age twenty-three, I traveled across the USSR as a Russian-speaking guide on an American exhibition, *Photography USA*. Created by the U.S. government under a cultural exchange agreement with the Soviets, the program was conceived at the height of the Cold War to counter disinformation against the West in general and the United States in particular. The goal was to encourage Soviet visitors to question the Kremlin's view of the world or to reinforce doubts about the storyline many already had.

The work of a guide was fascinating but grueling. It entailed standing six hours a day on the exhibit floor, fielding questions from a ceaseless flow of visitors: How much does a kilo of lard cost in America? What's the current unemployment rate? Who *really* killed JFK? In my early weeks on the stand, it quickly became apparent that I was speaking with a vast cross-section of Soviet people. Many were highly educated; others clearly were not. Their worldviews ranged from urbane to starkly provincial, across a spectrum from staunch believers in the Soviet system to closet dissidents.

One typical day, in Novosibirsk, I was out on the stand trying *not* to have a full-blown argument with a visitor loudly proclaiming America's faults. My job was to marshal some facts and figures and speak intelligently in Russian to rebut his most outlandish claims. By then, after six hours of similar exchanges, I was exhausted, physically and mentally—like a boxer in the twelfth round who could barely keep his arms up. My loud friend then launched into a new diatribe: America as an imperial, colonialist power. Before I could gather my wits to respond, a middle-aged man in the crowd broke in and harangued him: "You know *nothing* about America! The United States was historically an anti-colonialist nation!" He went on to detail the Revolutionary War, our support for decolonization after World War II—frankly, a more nuanced answer than I could have managed even in English.

After the loudmouth moved on, my rescuer silently smiled at me as if to say, "Don't worry about that idiot—we know the *real* score here." I never saw him again, and have no idea who he was. But it was an indelible moment, an early indication that this was a society and a people far more complex and multi-layered than most Americans—including, as it turned out, me—understood.

John Beyrle first went to Russia on a student exchange in 1976. His thirty-year career in the Foreign Service included three assignments to the U.S. Embassy in Moscow, beginning as a junior officer in 1983 and culminating as ambassador from 2008 to 2012. He also served as the U.S. ambassador to Bulgaria.

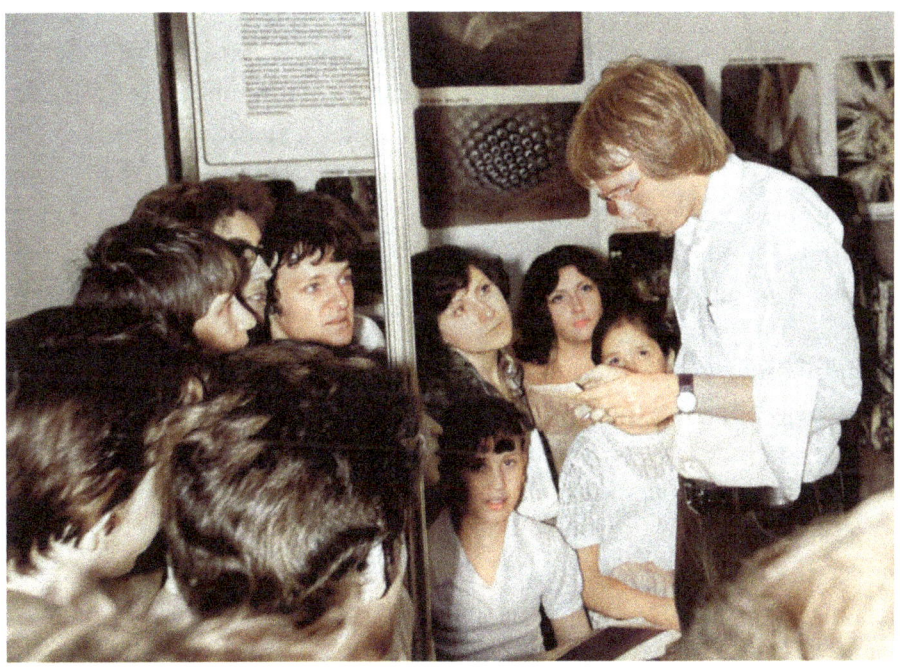

WE WANTED THE BEST
Alan Bigman

The Mil Mi-8 helicopter touched down at the collective farm *Red Stormtrooper*, near the village of Buturlino in Nizhny Novgorod Province, around 9:15 a.m. on a crisp spring day in April 1993. On board were some agricultural officials from the regional center—and two young Americans.

I was one of them. My job was "field manager" (that is, a junior person who doesn't get to commute back and forth to the United States) for the International Finance Corporation, the private sector arm of the World Bank. After tackling retail and trucking privatization, our team leader had decided to go after perhaps the most intractable problem of the Soviet economy—its collectivized agriculture. As a Russian studies and economics dual major, I had long marveled at the inefficiency of the Soviet command economy in general and its farm sector in particular. The Russian Empire had once been a major exporter of grain, while the Soviet Union spent precious hard currency importing foodstuffs from the West.

To design the program, we brought in top specialists from the Russian Academy of Agricultural Sciences, Russian legal experts, and advisers from other former socialist countries. We didn't write reports from Moscow or even from Nizhny Novgorod—we spent most of our time at the five farms selected as pilots for the land reform program.

We developed a model to distribute land and agricultural assets to collective farm members through an internal auction. No money changed hands—only their (until then, purely theoretical) ownership stakes in the collective.

The auctions turned out to be the heart of the program. They marked a moment of transition, a chance for people to decide their own destinies—a dramatic break with the past. By the third of our five auctions, Prime Minister Viktor Chernomyrdin arrived with more than fifty regional governors to witness a collective farm being privatized.

I will never forget that day. Boris Nemtsov, then governor of Nizhny Novgorod, explained that his foreigners were better than the Moscow ones—and had me recite a Russian *chastushka* (a short, rhymed Russian folk verse) to prove that we had gone somewhat native. Later, after the auction, Chernomyrdin rose, dramatically threw away his prepared remarks, and invited the Nizhny Novgorod team to Moscow to help draft a government decree to privatize all collective farms in Russia using our model.

That is, in fact, what happened—and within a few months, our mechanism became law across the country. Russia is once again a major grain exporter, though of course the results varied depending on implementation and local conditions. I might end by quoting one of Chernomyrdin's most famous sayings: "We wanted the best, but it came out as always."

Alan Bigman is a finance executive who spent more than a decade in Russia during the country's economic transition, where he helped lead the International Finance Corporation's pioneering program to privatize collective farms in the early 1990s. He later served in senior management roles, including director of corporate finance at TNK—one of Russia's largest oil companies and a predecessor to TNK-BP—working closely with Russian and Western partners. Since 2004, he has held senior finance positions in Western Europe and the United States, including serving as chief financial officer of LyondellBasell.

BEYOND THE PIPELINE
John Dabbar

Russian pipelines have long been a contentious and newsworthy subject, largely due to the geopolitical weight of oil and gas politics. The Russian crude oil export network, *Druzhba*, was initiated under the Council for Mutual Economic Assistance (Comecon), connecting the USSR to Eastern Europe. To this day, the Russian pipeline system remains a state-controlled enterprise.

The first privately operated pipeline, the Caspian Pipeline Consortium (CPC), was launched in the mid-1990s. By the spring of 1999, the CPC pipeline was under construction, and I was tasked with managing the commercial department. In addition to overseeing contracts, tariffs, laboratory quality, inventory control, and customs clearance, I was also responsible for building and leading the team that would operate both the pipeline and the marine terminal.

I hired the control room operators for the CPC operations center in Novorossiysk and developed their training program. Technical skill was essential—but it was only part of the equation. Many of our hires came from Transneft and the Russian Defense Ministry's Pipeline Directorate, bringing valuable experience. Still, we were unsure about cultural alignment. Would they take personal responsibility for 24/7 operations without direct supervision from one of the foreign investors' secondees? More importantly, if a technical problem suggested a potential leak or safety risk, would they have the authority—and the willingness—to shut down the pipeline?

To address these concerns, we brought the entire team to a pipeline operations center in Houston to observe best practices firsthand. To my surprise and delight, when the Russian and American pipeliners sat down together, they spoke a common language. Contrary to the conventional wisdom about the hierarchical structure of Russian labor, our Novorossiysk team displayed a level of confidence and personal accountability that genuinely impressed our American hosts.

We returned to Russia reassured. From that moment on, I had no doubt they could keep the oil flowing—or stop it, if necessary.

That confidence was tested in the summer of 2003. A flash flood in the Myskhako agricultural zone swept a campground of young people into the Black Sea, halting all shipping traffic, including operations at the CPC terminal. Our team responded swiftly and correctly, shutting down operations and helping ensure all the campers were safely rescued.

John Dabbar lived in Moscow for eleven years between 1996 and 2010. In addition to working for the Caspian Pipeline Consortium, he held positions in the Moscow offices of TNK-BP and ConocoPhillips. Before and after his time in Russia, he lived in Egypt, Japan, West Germany, Azerbaijan, and Kazakhstan.

BUILDING A LEGAL BRIDGE
Doran Doeh

In 1993, I was tasked with setting up Allen & Overy's Moscow office, and became its head in 1995, the culmination of a process set in motion earlier in the decade.

The fall of the Berlin Wall in 1989 was a geopolitical shockwave, whose full consequences took time to unfold. Major players in the West had to reassess their positions and chart new strategies. At Allen & Overy, one of London's leading law firms, the early 1990s recession prompted partners to look eastward. The firm initially focused on Czechoslovakia, Hungary, and Poland, where privatization and economic restructuring created an urgent demand for international legal expertise.

Russia, however, posed a far greater challenge. Seventy years of Communist rule had obliterated the remnants of an already fragile Tsarist-era legal tradition. A capitalist economy required a new legal framework, yet none existed. Fortunately, the Russian Constitution of 1993 provided a crucial foundation, mandating that no law could take effect unless published—eliminating the secrecy that had plagued both Tsarist and Soviet rule. The legislature moved swiftly, drawing from German, Dutch, and Swiss civil codes to rebuild the legal system.

Setting up a law office in this environment was daunting. Russia had no independent commercial law firms; legal work had been confined to ministries and state enterprises. Only major international firms entered the market, driven by clients eager to navigate the complexities of privatization. But finding local lawyers who met international standards—both in legal acumen and fluency in precise legal English—proved difficult. Competition for such talent was fierce.

At the time, Russian universities had not yet developed the specialized curricula needed to train commercial lawyers. Western firms had no choice but to immerse themselves in Russia's evolving legal landscape, learning alongside the few qualified Russian lawyers they could recruit. This created an unusual camaraderie among international firms—despite competing for business, they often supported one another in a way rarely seen elsewhere.

Those early years in Moscow were challenging yet formative. They laid the groundwork for Russia's modern legal system and cemented the role of international firms in its development. The experience of building a legal presence from the ground up remains one of the most dynamic chapters in my professional life.

Doran Doeh first visited Leningrad in 1990 and returned to Moscow in 1991, just before the collapse of the Soviet Union. Qualified as a barrister and a solicitor in England, he spent much of the following thirty years in Russia, representing in succession two of the leading and largest international law firms.

GORBI MANIA!
Hans Wicks

Looking at it now, I wince a little. The photograph was taken at Spaso House—the neoclassical residence of the American ambassador in Moscow—during the annual Fourth of July celebration. In it, I'm towering awkwardly over one of the twentieth century's giants: Mikhail Gorbachev. Worse still, my arm is slung casually around his shoulder, as though we were old college friends.

It wasn't a gesture of disrespect; I was simply starstruck. Just as my mother had once revered John F. Kennedy after his "*Ich bin ein Berliner*" speech, I had grown up seeing Gorbachev as a historical force cloaked in human vulnerability. Summoning my courage, I approached him, introduced myself as a Berliner and lifelong admirer (as many Berliners are), and asked for a photograph. He graciously obliged. The plastic cups in our hands suggest we had just shared a drink. In truth, we exchanged no more than five words. Still, I imagined my mother's reaction—me, of all people, standing beside him. Slightly embarrassing in retrospect. But in that moment, the small act of self-promotion seemed justified.

When I arrived in Russia a year earlier, I was comically unprepared. I had followed Soviet politics since the Brezhnev era, of course, but understanding headlines is one thing; understanding a nation's soul is quite another. Many impressions were difficult to process. There was the dignified old man in a threadbare suit, his shoes held together with Scotch tape, quietly waiting for a bus. Or the elderly taxi driver in his rattling Zhiguli who, upon learning I was German, pulled over with tears in his eyes. "My mother kept me home from school the day Stalin died," he whispered. "She said, 'Today, we mourn.'"

Such scenes stood in stark contrast to the gaudy, unrestrained consumerism flourishing in Moscow—where the poor and kindhearted existed side by side with the brash and empathy-devoid. Both, in their own way, seemed to be natural consequences of the same systemic collapse.

And amid all that, I was there—somehow. With no clear role, no obvious credentials. Yet positioned at the center of a moment that felt historic. Something my friends back home would only glimpse on CNN.

I often felt like an impostor, as if I'd stumbled into history's VIP section with the wrong name on the badge. And nothing captured that feeling better than the day I posed—arm a little too familiar—beside Gorbi himself.

Hans Wicks is a West Berliner who came to the United States as a child and studied at the University of California, Santa Barbara, and Stockholm University. His career took him to Denmark, Ireland, and the Netherlands, and to a long stint in Russia, where he headed Delta Air Lines for twenty-one years. He left after the start of the war in 2022.

DREAMS OF SARATOV
Thomas Fallows

My fascination with Russia began in the spirit of the 1960s: I came to see the high hopes crushed by the destructiveness of Bolshevism. I needed to explore not just ideology but the underlying forces that extinguished a liberal alternative during the Russian Revolution—I had to learn Russian to pursue answers.

What a thrill it was to hear *russkiy yazyk* (the Russian language) for the first time! I studied hard enough to be accepted as an exchange student from UC Berkeley to Leningrad State University in 1973. I was captivated. My dormitory life on Vasilevsky Island was rich with friendships—Gera, the KGB spy assigned as my roommate, and my Californian buddy Marilyn—both of whom were part of a memorable, chaotic night on the Dnieper in Kiev. I had a silent crush on Elena, the wife of another Leningrad friend, Valera.

As I entered graduate studies at Harvard University, my research turned to Russian landlord–peasant relations (with a focus on Saratov Province in the mid-Volga region). But the Soviets would not let me see Saratov: during my PhD research in Moscow in 1980–81, I was denied a domestic visa to go there. Back in the United States, I would literally dream of seeing the Volga and finally setting foot in Saratov.

I returned to Moscow (now Russia, not the USSR) in the mid-1990s for a two-week Citibank assignment. It was jarring to see impoverished babushkas begging on the streets as stretch limos ferried budding oligarchs past them. Yet it was heartening to see Russians beginning at last to emerge from the grip of state control.

At last, in 2013, my Saratov dream became reality. I finally saw the Volga with my own eyes. I traveled with a fellow Saratov specialist, and we stayed with Russian friends in a small village, spending the weekend in a Khrushchev-era housing complex known locally, and half-ironically, as the "Klondike." The highlight of my visit to Saratov was tracing the legacy of Stolypin, Lvov, Chenykaev, and other figures of the 1905 Revolution whose lives I had studied in Soviet archives three decades earlier. Standing before landmarks they once knew or that now commemorate them, walking their streets, and meeting young Russians there today felt like coming home—to a place I had never been, yet always carried in my heart.

My love for the Russian people is profound. Their generosity, humor, and resilience have left an indelible mark on me. And yet I am often struck by the cruelty of the system that has governed their lives—whether in the oppressive past or in its grim resurgence today.

Thomas Fallows lived in the USSR twice—Leningrad in 1973 and Moscow from 1979 to 1980—while pursuing a PhD in Russian history at Harvard. He later spent three decades in corporate and investment banking with Chase Manhattan and Citibank, followed by roles in asset management and investment advisory in Saudi Arabia. Now retired, he has taken up sailing in New York City.

AND THERE WAS LIGHT
Brook Horowitz

Moscow, 1995

The "Wild East" had set in. Widespread privatization of state property was underway, leading to the eventual rise of the oligarch class. It was "shock" without the "therapy."

At the time, I was on my second tour of duty in Moscow with General Electric (GE). My role was to rebuild the lighting business in the former Soviet Union—from distribution of lamps to potential mergers and acquisitions of Russian lighting manufacturers.

In the early 1990s, the streets of Moscow were a dingy affair. Old-tech, high-consumption mercury lamps—if they worked—cast a wan light on the city. Energy shortages were still commonplace. Although the entrepreneurial spirit had been unleashed, the public lighting remained unchanged.

When the Gore–Chernomyrdin Energy Efficiency Fund was launched, it provided just the opportunity that was needed. The Moscow City Center Lighting Project became one of the first initiatives supported by the fund.

The aim was to refit the entire center of Moscow within the Ring Road with energy-efficient sodium lamps. The project also introduced new ways of managing government contracts.

I led the GE bid, and we won it. This was not a simple project, but one fine day, we were ready for the official lighting ceremony. Tverskoi Bulvar was the venue. As dusk descended, Mayor Yury Luzhkov arrived—late—in his cavalcade. The moment had come. The TV lights were dimmed, the blaring Russian pop music silenced. We waited in suspense. We'd all worked in Russia long enough to know that a lighting ceremony was fraught with risk.

Mayor Luzhkov flicked the switch. Darkness. But then, in the gloom, the lamps flickered to life, emitted a dim glow, and grew steadily brighter. A collective sigh of relief. Moscow was bathed in a golden light—emblematic of this new period of reconstruction and collaboration.

The fixtures, all adorned with USAID's logo and the tagline "From the American People," lasted twenty-five years. As they were taken down at the end of their natural life, U.S.–Russia relations—never again to reach such dizzying heights—were being dismantled, too. We were perhaps naïve, but at the time, many of us were genuinely optimistic about the prospects for peace. Can we—and Russia—ever rekindle the belief we once had?

Brook Horowitz is the CEO of IBLF Global, an NGO that promotes responsible business practices in emerging and developing markets. In the 1990s, he held a variety of commercial positions with General Electric in Russia, Eastern Europe, and Western Europe.

MOSCOW'S FINEST
Brian Lee

It was December 2002 when the opportunity arose: an interview in Moscow with Ogilvy & Mather, the global advertising agency. They were seeking someone to lead their international clients in Russia. I was living in London at the time. After securing a visa, I was flown in to meet the team and, equally important, to sample the once-Soviet capital.

I arrived late on a Saturday night in January 2003. The hotel—Marriott Grand on Tverskaya—took my passport and kept it overnight for registration, a standard procedure. This meant that I wasn't leaving the hotel until the following morning, despite my eagerness to look around.

The next day, an English staff member, a recent arrival herself, offered to walk me to the Kremlin—a mere twenty minutes away. I was giddy. I'd glimpsed the onion domes the night before, but now I would see them in full, frostbitten glory.

It was a perfect Moscow winter morning: minus twenty Celsius, bone-dry air, sun like crystal. I had packed layers—long underwear, wool coat, scarf—but only one pair of shoes: polished leather, utterly unsuited for Russian snow.

Still, we walked down Tverskaya, through wet, slushy crossings and past snowbanks. Near Pushkinskaya, I was still warm but beginning to feel the chill creep into my shoes when we heard it: "Stop. Passport."

The Moscow *politsiya*.

Two obvious foreigners, speaking English, wearing dress shoes in January—we were easy prey. In moments, we found ourselves in the backseat of a tin-can police car, passports in hand, with no clue what was happening. They let us call the office. The woman on the line spoke quickly: "They want cash."

I had British pounds. My companion had U.S. dollars. In the front seat, the officers—who spoke no English—murmured to each other, tossing out words like *dollar*, *pounds*, and, unmistakably, *exchange rate*. One of them pointed toward a nearby currency exchange sign, its red digital rates glowing above the sidewalk. After a moment's deliberation, they decided: pounds it was.

Ten minutes later, we were lighter by £200, back on the street with our passports.

My companion turned to me. "You want to go back to London now? I'd understand."

"Are you kidding?" I grinned. "That was awesome. I've had more excitement in one Moscow morning than in twenty years of New York and London combined. Where do I sign?"

I stayed twelve years.

The Cold War story unraveled—undone by friendship, by kindness, by life itself.

Brian Lee has traveled to and from Russia since the mid-1990s. He lived and worked in Moscow from 2002 to 2014, leading country operations for two global advertising agency groups. He met his future wife, Natasha, there, and they have one daughter.

UTOPIA
Ambassador (Ret.) Michael Tay

This isn't about the Soviet vision of utopia, but another kind entirely—utopia as imagined by Russian composer Vladimir Martynov.

I first encountered Martynov's music at a 2004 concert featuring *Vita Nova* ("New Life"), his choral work. It was life-changing—my first plunge into the austere, soaring beauty of Russian choral tradition.

With some trepidation, I arranged to meet him. I wasn't sure what I would say. It marked my first real step into the beauty and complexity of the Russian soul.

He surprised me. His jacket was threadbare—an outward sign of humility. I had expected a worldly, aloof figure. Instead, he was disarmingly grounded. In a moment of boldness, I asked if he might compose a piece if I could find the funding. Almost a year passed before I returned to him with a plan.

I invited him and violinist Tatiana Grindenko—a formidable artist and presence—to Singapore, hoping it might inspire a modest chamber work. When I saw him again, he startled me: he would not write a quartet, but a full symphony.

He explained that he wasn't composing for a country, but for an idea—utopia. Not the Marxist-Leninist endpoint, but a Taoist concept: the "Way" that cannot be fully described. In Singapore, he sensed a society in constant evolution, a living embodiment of that idea. His vision was cross-civilizational and universal.

In another impulsive move, I asked him to add a choral dimension. He agreed. The result was a 100-person ensemble. The libretto drew from the *Tao Te Ching*. The music began with minimalist chant, folded in Asian instrumentation, and—at one point—wove in Schumann's "In Foreign Lands."

Fearing the piece would be too avant-garde, I avoided the early rehearsals. But just before the 2005 premiere at Tchaikovsky Concert Hall, I was persuaded to attend. I sat in the pews, quietly weeping—overcome by wonder, joy, and a touch of regret for having so misjudged it. It was a flight of spirit, surpassing anything I had imagined.

The London Philharmonic's 2019 recording of the Utopia Symphony carries the same transcendent force. Even now, as Russia enters another uncertain chapter, Martynov's music endures—proof that the Russian soul still reaches for light.

Michael Tay was the Singapore ambassador to Russia from 2003 to 2008. In addition to commissioning the symphony, he founded and led the Russia–Singapore Business Forum, a private-sector-driven conference that lasted eight years and forged an unprecedented relationship between a small nation and the largest country in the world.

EXPATS AND THE RUSSIA BALANCE SHEET
Andrew C. Kuchins

From 2003 to 2005, I served as director of the Carnegie Moscow Center (CMC), living in Moscow with my wife and our two young children. Despite having studied in Moscow in 1981 and returning more than forty times, this was my first time truly living there—with a family, a home, and a new perspective. That shift proved crucial. Previously, I had mostly interacted with Russians, but as a parent in the Anglo-American School community, I grew close to American and foreign professionals working in Moscow's private sector.

These individuals were a rich source of insight into how Russia really worked. Unlike policy analysts in Washington, they faced direct, high-stakes decisions, and their assessments of Russia's business and political climate were grounded in personal risk and financial consequence. Their views were often more sober. One example underscored the contrast: in Washington, Mikhail Khodorkovsky was viewed as a reformist; in Moscow's business circles, he was often regarded as ruthless, even criminal.

The timing complicated matters. Shortly before my arrival, the Carnegie Endowment had signed a contract to receive $1.5 million over three years from Yukos. After Khodorkovsky's arrest in October 2003, it felt as though a target had been painted on us. We were vilified—portrayed alternately as pawns of Khodorkovsky or, after the Beslan tragedy, as apologists for Chechen terrorism. By the end of 2005, we were locked in a desperate fight against NGO legislation that threatened to shutter CMC and many other foreign organizations.

I returned to Washington for Christmas that year physically and emotionally drained. It was the most challenging—and rewarding—job I had ever held. But what struck me most upon my return was how little the Washington discourse resembled the Russia I had just left. The press ignored the country's dynamic economic growth, which was reshaping society in real time. The narrative in policy circles was polarized and incomplete.

That gap in understanding led me to create the Russia Balance Sheet project, an effort to offer a more nuanced and accurate picture of Russia's political economy. For that, I remain grateful to the friends I made in Moscow—because if you want to understand a country, follow the money.

In addition to directing the Carnegie Moscow Center, Andrew Kuchins directed the Russia and Eurasia programs at the Carnegie Endowment for International Peace and later at CSIS in Washington. He was also president of the American University of Central Asia and now teaches at Johns Hopkins SAIS, where he also received his PhD.

II
CHANGE

We are no longer the same as we were yesterday.

Мы уже не те, что были вчера.

Ivan Turgenev, Fathers and Sons
Иван Тургенев, Отцы и дети
1860

THE JOURNEY THAT MATTERED
Steven Fisher

Moscow in midsummer: the air didn't stir, and neither did we. Cramped in a sweltering car inching out of the city, I was wedged between a kindred Cypriot spirit—my companion in many misadventures—and a Russian acquaintance whose name I've forgotten. We were bound for a supposedly upscale beach club near the Pirogovskoye Reservoir. No chilled drinks and shaded loungers yet—only the slow torture of a monumental traffic jam.

To pass the time, we stared out the windows. One block flaunted Stalinist neoclassical ambition—facades built to intimidate, stone heavy with intent. The next slipped into the dull uniformity of *Khrushchyovkas*, their chipped balconies and sagging lines telling a different story: grandeur and decay, side by side.

No one spoke. Fingers drummed against sunbaked glass. Eventually, the heat broke our silence: a muttered curse at the weather, another at the traffic, and then—inevitably—the talk turned to what it so often does in Russia: the fine art of things not working.

Somewhere in that shared exasperation, the mood shifted. I mentioned how, back in the U.S., people tend to tackle problems head-on. "If something's broken," I said, "you fix it." My Russian seatmate, with the offhand shrug of someone long acquainted with futility, offered another view: "Russians are more inclined to adapt to circumstances, recognizing that some things lie beyond our control. You wait. What else can you do?"

Maybe both approaches—change or acceptance—are just different routes to the same place. You still have to keep moving forward, even if the road is slow and uneven.

When I think of Russia, that conversation still rides in the back seat of my mind—wedged somewhere between frustration and quiet understanding.

We reached the beach club at last. The drinks were cold, the loungers shaded. But the real journey—the one that stayed with me—had already taken place, somewhere between motion and stillness, on a hot road out of Moscow.

Steven Fisher first visited the Soviet Union in 1983. From 2002 to 2010, based in Moscow, he led Citibank's corporate banking operations in Russia, Kazakhstan, and Ukraine, arranging major financings for domestic and international companies, and serving on the board of the American Chamber of Commerce in Russia. He now writes on Russia and its place in the world.

WARM WEST TO FRIGID EAST
Bryan Dougall

In the early 1990s, I left behind the golden sun of California and stepped into the steel-gray chill of Moscow—a city that, in those days, felt as cold emotionally as it was physically. Underdressed and overconfident, armed with a professional contract, I stepped into Moscow's subzero shock. I nearly got frostbite—twice. The streets offered no comfort: faces were serious, eyes guarded. What I had always assumed to be human nature—warmth, small talk, easy smiles—suddenly seemed like a cultural invention.

But the contract kept me tethered. And over the course of that first year, I began to perceive the depth beneath the surface: the poetry of the architecture, the silent endurance of the people, the way history seemed to hover in the air like smoke. And then there were the parties—decadent, unpredictable, and wildly alive.

In 1994, I experienced Russia's economic challenges firsthand when the ruble's value dropped significantly overnight, halving the worth of my recently converted savings. Friends explained why gold and foreign cars were considered safer investments than bank deposits. I learned quickly that in Russia, security was a fiction.

The workplace proved equally revealing. I encountered business practices that would have been unthinkable back home—deals struck in whispers, contracts honored only when convenient. But where there was dysfunction, there was also possibility. A friend and I, inspired by the city's raw nightlife, decided to open a bar. We called it The Hungry Duck.

It was a madhouse—a fraternity party without the pretense of higher education. Night after night, expats and locals poured in to dance, to drink, to disappear. For a time, it was the best job I've ever had: nine in the morning until seven the next, and never the same crowd twice. Until the Chechens showed up, and we learned that even chaos has its predators.

I moved on to other ventures, opening venues and pursuing opportunities across industries. Along the way, I realized that human talent, not natural wealth, was Russia's greatest resource.

Years passed. I stayed. I've driven, railed, and flown across this country's immense landscapes—from imperial cities to forgotten towns. I built a life and watched Russia transform—painfully, but unmistakably.

Even now, with tensions high and headlines grim, I remain—not because it's easy but because it's a place of opportunity and community, a place where connections are meaningful, and beauty is appreciated in everything.

Russia taught me to look deeper, wait longer, and to find warmth in places that first felt impossibly cold.

Bryan Dougall studied economics at the University of Southern California and went on to lead ventures ranging from Moscow nightlife (Hungry Duck, Le Club) to media, construction, and technology across Russia and the UAE.

RUSSIA'S "ANNÉES FOLLES"
Hadrien Fraissinet

Unlike many foreigners I met in Moscow, my family had no ties to the Russian Empire or the Soviet Union. My fascination with Russia likely stemmed from Ian Fleming's film adaptations. As a child, I kept asking, "Why are they so evil?" Seeking answers, I minored in Russian studies. There were only three of us—most students saw little value in a bankrupt country run by oligarchs.

Winter 2003. When Rothschild & Co. sought volunteers to open a Moscow office, I raised my hand. With barely two years of banking experience, I already knew that a steady diet of Excel, PowerPoint, and face time would kill me. In hindsight, my superiors likely felt the same and were relieved by my initiative. I craved something more exciting, more alive, less scripted. Little did I know I was embarking on a decade-long adventure.

Armed with four semesters of *russkiy yazyk* and naïve enthusiasm, Moscow greeted me with a slap. People were rude, nobody spoke English, and I struggled to decipher Muscovites. Poor infrastructure and gridlocked traffic made navigating the city a nightmare. Escaping the megalopolis on weekends was a test of will.

Yet not all was grim. Compared to my colleagues in London and Paris, my freedom was immense. We spent most of our time outside the office, pitching "synergies." Workdays began at 10:00 a.m. instead of 8:00, leaving two precious hours for Moscow's legendary nightlife. Beyond the opulent clubs, I fondly recall smoky evenings in Café Mayak and Petrovich. Among that bohemian intelligentsia, one could imagine Hemingway in the corner, changing the world one bottle at a time.

In 2005, Mikhail Lomtadze hired me at Baring Vostok Capital Partners. This was my most formative experience: "becoming" a shareholder. There was no better crash course in the realities of business than working at a leading private equity house. I admired Russian entrepreneurs—their ingenuity, relentless drive, and high tolerance for risk and failure, reminiscent of the American spirit. The sky was the limit, and Moscow's dynamism was unrivaled.

By 2009, the tide had turned. The West had overindulged on cake, yet Russia woke up with diabetes. The feverish optimism of the 2000s faded. Western commitment fell short of Russian expectations. The prodigal state rose from its ashes. Expats gave way to repats, liberals to siloviki. Game over. Anticipating my obsolescence, I made my exit in 2013.

Russia's magnetism ebbs and flows. She gives much—and takes as much back.

After a stint at the International Finance Corporation, Hadrien Fraissinet founded Qantara Capital, a private investment and advisory company, in 2015. He still practices his Russian and remains active in Kazakhstan, where he served on the board of KazTransOil—the national oil pipeline company—from 2019 to 2024.

THE METRO TOUR
Brian Zimbler

On a wintry morning in 1990, Dmitry introduced me to the Moscow Metro. An intense journalist for a Soviet newspaper, he dreamed of joining the emerging private sector. We entered Park Kultury station, passing pensioners selling spoons, plates, and other remnants of a fading era.

Through the heavy metal-and-glass doors, we descended a long corridor. Dmitry warned me to pass carefully through the toll gates; if one was too slow, metal barricades would swing out and smash your kneecaps. We stepped onto a long, dimly lit escalator, monitored by elderly women in small glass booths. At the bottom, we navigated the dense throng toward the platforms. The trains arrived with clockwork precision. Apart from the hum and screech of metal, the station was eerily silent.

We visited several stations adorned with grand statues and murals. Dmitry spoke with pride of the Soviet workers who built this vast network in the 1930s. It was a marvel of engineering, a symbol of collective achievement.

Later, in Dmitry's cramped flat, I met his wife and young daughter. Over vodka, we discussed the upheavals of *perestroika*. He confessed his bewilderment: How could the same system that built the Metro, defeated the Germans, and sent the first man into space be unraveling? How would his family survive if the economy collapsed? His deep uncertainty contrasted sharply with the pride he had shown earlier, leaving me disquieted. Was the country on the brink of chaos, or would reforms prevail? Could foreigners do business here? Would we be safe? Did we have a role to play?

Twenty-five years later, Moscow had become my home and the center of my professional life. Once again, I descended into the Metro, this time as the guide, leading a visiting American colleague.

I found myself back on my tour with Dmitry, and pondered the hopeful certainty I once mistook for understanding. The Soviet Union was gone. Its symbols were buried—or rebranded. Yet the city remained unsettled, familiar and strange all at once. The questions Dmitry once asked—about survival, direction, meaning—still hovered, unanswered. The Metro still ran on time. But above ground, the city moved differently—restless, unresolved.

Brian Zimbler served as a foreign lawyer in Moscow from 1994 to 2017, splitting his time between Moscow and London after 2000.

STREET SMART
Kira Gruger

A city reveals itself through the rhythm of its roads. As a thirteen-year-old, I arrived in Moscow expecting something like Prague, where I had lived for two and a half years—cobblestones, Gothic arches, fairy-tale charm.

Instead, I found Moscow's imposing urban grandeur. Ordinary streets stretched eight lanes wide, and the Seven Sisters skyscrapers cast long shadows over the city. Gray high-rise apartments loomed over the ring roads. It was on these streets that Moscow's personality came to light: quirky charms, like summertime vendors hawking massive watermelons in metal cages along the roadside, juxtaposed with the darker realities of crooked cops and rubles tucked between documents.

But to understand Moscow is to know its traffic. Living there felt like a daily negotiation between oneself and the city's sprawling arteries. Getting to school on time became a daily gamble. Leave at 7:00 a.m., and you might arrive ten minutes early—or miss everything. The roads were not only congested but also governed by traffic rules that were often more like suggestions. Our driver sometimes swerved onto the tram tracks, shaving off a few precious minutes. Even with its vast public transport, I often sat stalled in bumper-to-bumper traffic—watching the clock, going nowhere.

I have not lived in Moscow in decades. Most of my memories have faded, and the places I once knew have been replaced by restaurants, routines, and storefronts I would not recognize today. Yet the streets remain etched in my mind—vivid and chaotic. They were more than just a way of getting somewhere; they were where the city revealed itself—its contradictions, its pulse, its truths. What endures is not the traffic itself but the transformation it demanded: learning how to move through a city so vast and unyielding taught me how to navigate challenges larger than myself. And so, even as landmarks blur and languages shift, it is the memory of those roads that still moves with me.

Kira Gruger lived in Moscow for four years, attending the Anglo-American School of Moscow for high school. She is an ex-third culture kid who now lives in sunny Los Angeles, California.

SO MANY WINDOWS
Rachel Polonsky

In October 1999, we moved our family from Tverskaya Street to Romanov Pereulok. We loved the fact that the new apartment had been spared an *evroremont*, a 1990s-style renovation, and had kept its century-old parquet floors, molded cornices, and ceiling-high tiled stoves. Its double windows had not been replaced with the plastic *eurowindows* that had appeared all over the city. Their wooden frames were mostly sealed shut with scaly craquelure paint, but the small ventilation windows, called *fortochki*, still opened efficiently. The heavy iron radiators, like the rest of Moscow's infrastructure, looked sure to withstand the millennium bug that was on everyone's mind.

Our genial landlord, Aleksandr Aleksandrovich—known to all as San Sanich—was ready for some *remont*, however, and we agreed on a budget for updating the Soviet-era bathrooms and kitchen. "Everything to the client's taste," he insisted, "contemporary, *evropeiskii*." Over several weeks, San Sanich and I roamed the outskirts of Moscow together, hailing gypsy cabs and seeking out kitchen units and bathroom *santekhnika*. "Good day, comrade," he would say to the sales assistant with an outstretched hand as we entered a showroom. "We are doing a *remont*." "Vo! Impeccable taste!" he would chuckle as I picked out some inoffensive white tile or sink unit imported from Turkey.

Until 1989, San Sanich had been deputy chairman of the Presidium of the Supreme Soviet of the USSR. As I discovered when reading his obituary in 2018, he was born in the Kingdom of Romania in 1934, spent the first fifteen years of his career working in a tractor factory in Soviet Kishinev (now Chişinău), before rising through the Moldavian Communist Party ranks and reaching Moscow in time for perestroika.

One afternoon, stuck in traffic on the Garden Ring, we heard a news item on the radio about the Taliban in Afghanistan and someone called Osama bin Laden. "I flew into Kabul under gunfire once with a government delegation," San Sanich said with a conspiratorial smile. "Ah, those were interesting times."

We lived in the apartment for almost nine years. Occasionally, the telephone would ring for San Sanich. "This is the embassy of the Democratic People's Republic of Korea," a caller announced one day. The North Korean diplomat asked me to pass on an invitation to a national day celebration: "He was always an honored guest at our parties, an excellent guest," he said with warmth.

San Sanich was an excellent landlord, too.

Rachel Polonsky first visited the USSR in 1980. She studied in Leningrad in 1990–91 and lived in Moscow from 1998 to 2008 and again in 2017–18. She is the author of Molotov's Magic Lantern: a Journey in Russian History *(2010).*

KAIF
Michael Pugh

The alarm wrenched me from a vivid dream. I was trying to close a deal, despite two of my lawyers being signed off sick. Outside, Old Arkhip was already scraping the pavement clear of snow. Inside my flat, it was stifling.

It was Saturday, but I leapt out of bed. After a shower, followed by tea and a *vatrushka* (warm, round pastry) heavy enough to sink the Titanic, I nearly ran down the worn stairs of my stairwell and opened the front door of my building. The icy blast that hit my face was refreshing. Around Patriarshiy Prudy, the vintage lampposts cast a golden glow through the silvery dawn mist, lending the quiet streets an ethereal charm.

I heaved a sigh of relief as my Range Rover's V8 purred to life, the deep rumble promising escape. The drive out of Moscow carried me past the toytown entrance to the zoo, the statues of 1905's triumphant Russian heroes, and over Serebryany Bor, where warmly clad fishermen dotted the frozen river.

Retro FM played a cheery compilation of cheesy '80s hits as I sped westward. An hour and a half later, I turned off Minskoe Shosse at the sculpture of a Yak-3 fighter plane, frozen in mid-flight. Gradually, the concrete tower blocks of Mozhaisk gave way to village houses painted deep green and powder blue, their intricate fretwork laced with frost. Cresting a bluff brought me to the golden domes of Luzhetsky Monastery, gleaming against a sky so brilliantly blue.

Dogs rushed up to greet me as I left the car and made my way toward a barn outside, where men in eighteenth-century riding dress stood smoking.

"Michael, *privet!*" boomed Dima, resplendent in green velvet and gold brocade.

Inside, the women were visions of a bygone age, adorned in fur-trimmed brocade coats and voluminous gowns of crimson, gold, and damask blue. Tables groaned under steaming copper samovars and plates piled high with pancakes, red caviar, and thick sour cream.

"Michael, *privet!*" shouted Lyuba as she brought me a glass of hot, sweet black tea and a warm embrace.

Soon after, we mounted our horses before knocking back vodka from silver goblets. The horses jostled for position in clouds of hot breath as we left the stable yard. On reaching the open silence of the snow-covered meadows, the horses broke into a wild gallop, their hooves sending flurries into the pristine air.

"Kaif!" (bliss!)—shouted Lyuba as she raced past, her horse kicking up a spray of white powder that stung my face.

"*Kaif, voooobshe!*" I roared, spurring my horse onward, the thrill of the chase surging through my veins.

Michael Pugh is a lawyer, academic, writer, and founder of the Llangwm Literary Festival. He first visited Russia as a student in 1992, and his book about leaving Russia by horse, Riding through War and Peace, *will be published by Quiller in July 2026.*

CROSSING TVERSKAYA
Michael Tappan

On a Friday evening in late May 1998, my driver Anatoly maneuvered our way home through sluggish Moscow traffic. A hot, dry wind from the Siberian steppes blew grit through the car windows. At last, in my apartment in Pushkinskaya, I poured myself a gin and tonic, fell into my chair, and turned on CNN. With no plans for the evening, I decided to go out for a cheeseburger and a beer at the nearby TGI Friday's on Tverskaya Street.

From the restaurant's second-floor entrance, I saw two women across the room, sitting together at the bar. Not averse to a chance for conversation, I slipped onto a stool beside them and introduced myself. As we talked, Irina, who sat between me and her friend Tatiana, gradually became less shy and began asking questions in her limited English. Loquacious by my second beer, I told her I was an American in the executive-search business in Moscow with Russian partners. Wanting to make a good impression, I explained that our work in building a free market for management talent would eventually benefit Russia and its people. What a pathetic gambit, I thought—yet for me it was true. How much Irina understood, I wasn't sure.

By ten o'clock, Tatiana had left. I had never gotten around to ordering the cheeseburger, so I invited Irina for dinner at Scandinavia, a lively restaurant just on the other side of Tverskaya. Out on the sidewalk, over the roar of passing traffic, we could hear raucous shouting in the pedestrian passageway beneath the street. After all the beers, I felt unsteady at the top of the dimly lit stairway. Irina moved beside me and firmly took my arm, pulling me close. We descended the steps, wove through the drunken melee in the tunnel, and climbed the steps on the other side, still arm in arm. This young Russian woman's steady, caring hand warmed my spirit with unexpected force. Fate had struck, and I knew I was in big trouble.

Irina and I married in a Moscow "Wedding Palace" for foreigners in 2001 and have lived in the U.S. since 2003 with our three Moscow-born daughters. The city we knew has vanished, along with hope for a free and prosperous future for the Russian people. Despite all disappointments and unfulfilled goals as Russia sank into authoritarianism and war, that lucky meeting more than twenty-five years ago changed everything for me and resonates happily in my life and memory.

Michael Tappan was a cofounder and served as chairman of Ward Howell International in Russia beginning in 1992. He later lived in Moscow from 1998 to 2003. After retiring from Ward Howell in 2003, he returned to the United States and continued executive-search work in Russia as an affiliate of RSR Partners until 2013. He then rejoined Ward Howell International, where he specializes in supervisory and management board search projects in Ukraine.

THE FOUND ONE
Jennifer Neufeld

I found Naida on a tram in snowy St. Petersburg. I had just arrived to work at a small ad agency branch, feeling like an alien in a beautiful, bewildering land. A dirty auburn dog wandered from passenger to passenger, sniffing at the scent of *kolbasa* wafting from worn plastic bags. I took her home.

Naida—the found one—became my steady companion through a decade of change. She opened a door into Russian life I could never have entered on my own. At the time, foreigners were still a curiosity. But Naida made me familiar. Approachable. I was simply Naida's *Amerikanka*.

Russia was a land of contradictions: brutal winters and overflowing summers, fierce and tender, wary and welcoming. There were no acquaintances, only strangers or family. Naida helped me cross that divide.

There was the former Bolshoi dancer in the park, whose grandson played with Naida while we talked. She still carried herself like a queen. She shared soup recipes, whispered advice about Russian men, and somehow produced theater tickets out of thin air. There was my upstairs neighbor, her face often puffy, sometimes bruised after nights when shouting kept me awake and Naida on edge, who said little but sat silently while Naida rested her head on her knee. And there were the parents at the playground—once good communists, now told to be good capitalists—whose jokes were brittle and whose pride and anger were heartbreakingly raw.

One summer evening, after a bath, Naida slipped through the apartment door and vanished into the Moscow night. For days I searched. I mobilized my PR agency, distributed flyers, and organized search teams. I offered a thousand-dollar reward—a fortune at the time. Calls poured in, some sincere, others dangerous. After one frightening encounter in a deserted lot, I hired two ex-soldiers to meet callers instead. A friend appeared on television, and the story of the *Amerikanka* with the lost dog became national news.

Weeks later, the phone rang. A young woman's voice, calm and certain: "I think I have your dog." Across the city, there she was—Naida. Clean and well fed, she had been on the streets only a short time before the girl took her in. Inside her small, worn apartment, it was clear she had little. When I tried to press the reward into her hands, she shook her head—*ne nado*. No need. I left it behind anyway. She lived with little, but had given without hesitation. In a city hardened by survival, kindness still found a way.

The great Russian soul was too vast for me ever to fully understand. But for a time, together with Naida, I was allowed to belong.

Jennifer Neufeld arrived in Russia in 1993 for an internship with a small, curious Russian company with offices in the Hotel Orlyonok. Over the next thirteen years, she worked at ad agencies and eventually co-founded a strategic communications firm, whose first office was in the State Historical Museum, address: One Red Square. She left Russia in 2004 but sometimes swears she's still waiting for the next tram.

KITCHEN TABLE WISDOM
Daniel Satinsky

In the early 1990s, I went to study Russian in Yaroslavl, an industrial city founded in 1010 at the confluence of the Volga and Kotorosl Rivers, 180 kilometers northeast of Moscow.

On my first bus ride there from Moscow for a language immersion program, our Russian host told us, "Moscow is not Russia." Sayings like this pepper Russian speech and reflect commonly held truths. Over the course of my years working across Russia, I came to understand the depth of that statement. It became the second-most important saying about Russia I would come to know.

Years later, as a partner in a business center in Yaroslavl, I visited frequently to promote our venture. After one reception, I found myself drinking with a vice-governor of Yaroslavl *Oblast*, whom I had never met before. We sat at a picnic table outside a local café. Around 3:00 a.m., he had his driver take us to his apartment, where his wife made us breakfast, and we continued our conversation nearly until dawn. The topics ranged from how Russians hunt wild boar to comparisons of political systems.

Late that night—or early that morning—as the conversation turned philosophical, he said something that has stayed with me ever since and became a touchstone in my thinking about Russia. It wasn't exactly an epiphany, but rather a practical guideline, as such sayings often are. He put it simply: "In the U.S., business is more important than politics. In Russia, politics is more important than business." I can't fully explain why it stuck with me, but I've found it useful ever since.

More than the words, what stays with me is the setting—hearing an insightful axiom from a man I never saw again, shared around a kitchen table in the middle of the night. It captured something of the mystery, hospitality, and emotional depth that defined so many such gatherings—and that remains one of my most vivid memories of Russia.

Daniel Satinsky first visited the Soviet Union in 1984 and began working in a pioneering American–Russian joint venture in 1990. He was involved in a range of business and consulting projects across Russia until 2014. From 1998 to 2014, he served as president of the board of the U.S.–Russia Chamber of Commerce of New England. He is the author of two books on American–Russian relations from the 1980s to the 2000s, most recently Creating the Post-Soviet Russian Market Economy: Through American Eyes.

NO MORE BREAD LINES
Meena Mylvaganam

Moscow changed my life in ways I could never have imagined.

Our tiny house on the tropical island of Singapore is filled with Russian memorabilia—from the contemporary art hanging on our walls (including our daughter's eighth-grade art project, bought at a fundraiser at the now-closed Anglo-American School—shut down by the Russian government); to Art Deco furniture from the *komissiya* (комиссия) in our neighborhood; to Lomonosov coffee cups and the myriad tchotchkes from the "antiques"/junk market at Izmailovo.

For six years, we lived just minutes from Red Square, on Romanov Pereulok, and I never tired of seeing St. Basil's onion domes—from the first time I set eyes on them that wintry morning we arrived in January 2003 to the summer's day we left in August 2008.

The idea of living in Russia thrilled me beyond words. I had studied Soviet politics at university, having been introduced to Tolstoy and Solzhenitsyn in my teenage years by my teacher father.

At the first event my husband and I hosted at our embassy to introduce ourselves to the small Singaporean community, a man asked, "Are you Mr. Myle's daughter?" When I said I was, he was thrilled to tell me what an impact my father had made on his life and how he had come to work in Russia as an engineer because of him. I thought he was going to cry when I told him my father had passed away about five years earlier.

When I told my mother that my husband had been posted to Russia as Singapore's ambassador, a stricken look crossed her face. I said, "They no longer stand in bread lines, you know." And she replied, "Oh, okay." In fact, by the time we left, they did stand in line—again. This time, it was at the French bakery Volkonsky—for croissants and macarons to rival Sprüngli in Zurich or Ladurée in Paris.

The Moscow we left was not the one we had arrived in. The city had changed—more modern, more extravagant, more uncertain. So had we. The experience had seeped into the fabric of our daily lives, and there was no going back. Moscow, in all its contradictions, had made itself at home in us.

Meena Mylvaganam is a book editor who lived in Moscow from 2003 to 2008, where she was the co-chair of the International Women's Club's charity wing. She was active in the arts scene, including commissioning a symphony on Singapore by Russian composer Vladimir Martynov and organizing multiple art exhibitions at the Embassy of Singapore to showcase the work of Russian contemporary artists.

GOING BANANAS
Robert Stephenson

In the early 1990s, after the collapse of the Soviet Union, Russian citizens experienced a wave of excitement and joy as long-lost pleasures returned to shops and markets. Over decades, a wide variety of foods had gradually disappeared from everyday diets, becoming either luxuries available only to the Soviet elite or rare treats most people could only dream about. When the country transitioned to a market economy, however, the floodgates opened, and these once-familiar items began to reappear on store shelves, in markets, and in the windows of new kiosks springing up across towns and cities.

For Western visitors working daily alongside their Russian counterparts, this change became a feature of everyday life. It was common for Russian colleagues to arrive at the workplace proudly displaying the day's discoveries. These might include bottles of Moldovan brandy or Georgian wine—beverages many had not seen in decades, which inspired both nostalgia and hope for better times. But it was not only alcohol that sparked joy. The reappearance of imported fruits—especially bananas—was a true cause for celebration. Bananas had become virtually impossible to find in Soviet times, reserved for special occasions or smuggled in from abroad. Now, with the shift toward an open market, they—and other exotic fruits—arrived in abundance, and people could not get enough.

As a keen photographer, my eyes were drawn to an overflowing garbage bin outside Gorky Park on a late Sunday afternoon in the summer of 1992. The resulting image provides a visual reminder of how, in the 1990s, bananas became the snack of choice—consumed with abandon, as if people were trying to make up for all the years they had been denied this simple pleasure. The joy was not just about the fruit itself but about the freedom that came with the choice to buy it at all. It was a taste of a world beyond the long lines and empty shelves that had once defined daily life.

The return of these foods—and other lost pleasures—was a powerful symbol of change. It meant that people no longer had to rely on black-market deals or go without. Now there was a sense of plenty—an exciting contrast to the years of scarcity. For Russians in the early 1990s, the sudden availability of these goods was a reminder—amid the economic and social hardships of transition—of the new possibilities and freedoms that the country's dramatic turn had offered.

Looking back now, that moment feels even sharper—a brief, heady time when the future seemed open, and even a banana tasted like hope.

Robert Stephenson first visited the Soviet Union in 1985. As a UK civil servant, he lived in Moscow from 1992 to 1997, working with the Federal Employment Service and other Russian ministries on a range of knowledge-sharing and capacity-building projects and programs. After returning to the United Kingdom, he continued to lead UK government and EU projects on public administration reform in Central and Eastern Europe.

MY FIRST JOB
John Stavis

June 1992 in Moscow was all sunshine, picnics at Serebryany Bor, and no sunscreen required.

One week later, in Raduzhny, Western Siberia, it was snowing and windy, and I was ankle-deep in mud and sand. How did I get here?

White Nights was among the first oil-production joint ventures between American and Russian partners. I had been hired as a kind of jack-of-all-trades, which was probably all I was qualified for, given that I had no marketable skills at age twenty-four—other than my native English, strong Russian language skills, and a willingness to go places like Raduzhny.

There were generally two types of foreign employees at White Nights: oilfield professionals in their fifties and sixties, prone to heart attacks and the temptation of young, attractive Russian women; and wastrels like me. A colleague, Dan, was a typical example of the latter. One fine day, Dan borrowed the general director's car without permission to visit his girlfriend—who, at that time, was also the general director's driver's girlfriend—at the sauna. On the way there, a massive eight-wheel Uragan off-road missile carrier—used to transport oilfield equipment—T-boned him at an intersection, totaling the car. Dan walked away unscathed but unfulfilled.

One of my many responsibilities was to cover for the administrative director at the production site when he was on home leave. Traveling to Raduzhny was always an adventure. The usual method was by charter jet that seemed to get lost, then flew around vast areas of the Siberian taiga under the clouds while the navigator traced gridlines on a map and looked straight down through the glass nose of the aircraft, trying to find the airstrip.

On this particular trip, I had to organize a field visit for the elders of the Khanty tribesmen, who owned the surface rights to our drilling concession. We spent four hours shivering in the cold—why bring a winter coat in June?—visiting the various drilling sites, where violation after violation was noted: berms too low to contain tailings, dogs on site (they harass the reindeer), drainage issues, trash strewn around, and so on. After two hours of dressing-down from the Khanty, I finally began to understand the true depths of my innocent incompetence. Lesson learned—Russia doesn't care if you think it's June.

John Stavis graduated from Brown University in 1989 with a degree in Russian and history. He worked in Russia for the White Nights joint venture from 1991 to 1994. He continues to speak Russian daily with his wife, Irina—Russia's best-ever export.

MASTERING THE ART OF COOKING IN MOSCOW
Jennifer Eremeeva

I miss little about Moscow.

Not the traffic jams, nor the menacing encounters with bureaucrats, nor the creeping hostility toward foreigners that spread like an invasive blight after 2014.

But I miss my markets.

I learned about food while navigating three of Moscow's sprawling farmers markets: Leningradsky, Dorogomilovsky, and Danilovsky. Each market represented a stage in my development, from cautious amateur cook to confident food writer. I tentatively probed Leningradsky as a new mother in search of fresh produce for baby food. I braved Dorogomilovsky during the expansive years of the early aughts, joining Moscow's chefs in search of exotic and hard-to-find ingredients such as cockles and lovage.

Toward the end of my time in Moscow, I turned to Danilovsky to document efforts to create European-style markets—like Barcelona's Mercat de la Boqueria or London's Borough Market—in Moscow. By this time, my hobby had morphed into a profession: I was a food writer, documenting the hipsters flocking to Danilovsky to indulge in pho, smash burgers, and gourmet pelmeni.

A visit to any market always got my creative juices flowing. I usually arrived with a vague plan, but more often than not, the list stayed in the pocket of my coat as I navigated the market aisles, amidst the cacophony of rumbling carts and shouts in the languages of the former Soviet Union. Before buying anything, I happily accepted samples of impossibly sweet homemade raspberry preserves, velvety smoked fish, and bracingly sour pickles.

As the years turned into decades, my culinary ambitions expanded and my confidence grew. By the end of my time in Moscow, I could clean and tie superb beef tenderloins—sold at a hard-to-find kiosk tucked behind the Dorogomilovsky parking lot—with ease, all while listening to podcasts detailing Russia's steady slide into authoritarianism.

I didn't come to Moscow to be a cook or a writer, but that's what I became—and the markets were my training grounds. Food in Moscow was a puzzle: where to find the missing ingredients, how to substitute tools that weren't available, and how to turn lackluster recipes into vibrant dishes full of flavor. Inscrutable puzzles, to be sure, but ones with solutions—unlike so many problems outside the markets and my Moscow kitchen. Corruption in the kitchen could be banished with a generous spray of Mr. Proper.

I miss my markets.

Jennifer Eremeeva is a travel and food writer and cruise ship enrichment lecturer based in Riga, Latvia. She explores the intersection of culture, history, and cuisine in major travel destinations through her lectures, books, and newsletter Destination Curation. *She is the award-winning author of two books:* Lenin Lives Next Door: Marriage, Martinis, and Mayhem in Moscow *and* Have Personality Disorder, Will Rule Russia: A Pocket Book of Russian History. *Contact: solo.to/jennifereremeeva.*

A CAPITAL PERSPECTIVE
Guy Archer

June 2000, Blue Ridge Mountains, Virginia
At a wedding reception, a University of Virginia law dean asks me, in all sincerity, if I have to queue for toilet paper in Moscow.

His question—innocent, curious—hands me the missing piece for the magazine I'm building with my business partner.

I've spent two years in Moscow, and we're launching a small publishing house. Our flagship: *Capital Perspective*, a glossy cultural magazine exploring Moscow and Russia, later with a section promoting foreign investment. But until now, I hadn't quite grasped our audience. His question makes it clear: highly educated, globally engaged foreigners who know next to nothing about contemporary Russia. They have no idea how vibrant, promising, and endlessly surprising the country has become. But they want to know, I'm sure; they need to know.

2000–2002, Moscow
As *Capital Perspective*'s cofounder and editor, with the most creative team I've worked with—or ever will—we produce unwieldy, graphically arresting, brilliant, and intelligent magazines every two months. Some serious riffing about or by Moscow Conceptualists here, Troika Dialog analysis there, some good, solid architectural or art history layered throughout.

For two years, the magazine thrives, winning praise in Russia and abroad. But we're fighting a losing battle. Print is already falling to the Internet, and our feverish enthusiasm would dull the moment we truly learned what we were doing. Growth means change, and Moscow is changing. So in 2002, we shut down, dividing the remnants—office chairs, computers, memories.

2002–2022, Moscow
I stay. More or less. I'm communications director for the American Chamber of Commerce in Russia for seven years. I begin another niche publishing company. Every once in a while, I move away; but I always

come back to Moscow. I know this is where I belong—in my city, still seeing some hope, though vanishing.

January 1, 2025, Kyiv
In the early hours of New Year's Day, a Russian drone attack rattles my apartment. Down the street, debris crashes against buildings. Everyone knew they would strike today, just as they had on Christmas.

I'm sometimes aware of a weird, dead look in my eyes as I think about my magazine.

Guy Archer is president and cofounder of New Gauge Initiative, a U.S.-based nonprofit focusing on the modernization of Ukraine's railway infrastructure. He cofounded the Moscow Architecture Preservation Society in 2004. He lives part-time in Odesa and, quixotically, continues to pursue publishing about cultural projects in his spare time.

OUR HOME IN MOSCOW
Jim Balaschak

My wife and I moved to Moscow in the spring of 1995, joining the wave of expatriates eager to explore opportunities in the new Russia. But where could we live? At the time, a proper real estate market was virtually nonexistent. Our first living quarters were off Leningradsky Prospect, on the fourth floor of a decaying Soviet hotel—a decidedly short-term arrangement.

Finding a suitable apartment proved to be an arduous task. We toured dozens of places, usually located through a labyrinthine network of referrals. At last, we secured an apartment near my office. A one-year lease was signed, and the deal was sealed with champagne, chocolates, and heartfelt toasts.

The twelve-story building, located on Petrovsko-Razumovskaya Allee, was one of the *Khrushchyovka* structures built after the war. It was long and rectangular, constructed from the ubiquitous tan brick seen all over the city. The building housed retired Russian army generals. Secure? Press one button, and the militia would arrive in less than two minutes. We liked that.

Our apartment was on the eighth floor. It had two doors: the outer one made of steel, and the inner one padded on the inside like a Chesterfield sofa. By Russian standards, it was spacious—approximately 150 square meters. Known as a "three-room" apartment, it featured a living and dining area, a bedroom, and a multipurpose room. There was a bathroom and a very small kitchen. Our balcony overlooked Dinamo Stadium.

But there were no modern appliances. Welcome back to the 1950s! No washing machine: clothes were scrubbed in the tub and hung on the balcony. No vacuum: sweep and mop. The dark oven barely accommodated our first Thanksgiving turkey roaster.

The decor reflected decades of wear. Linoleum peeled from the floors, and the furniture, though functional, was of poor quality. Two dining room chairs broke under guests on that first Thanksgiving. Security had triumphed over aesthetics.

Our landlord, General Bograd, was a retired army officer. His wife, a physician, added to their dignified air. This apartment had been his reward for years of service. A thoughtful and gentle man, he had served as a major in World War II and met the Americans at the Elbe—just as my father had met the Russians there.

Had they met? The possibility filled me with wonder as I imagined two young men, separated by language and ideology, unknowingly crossing paths at a pivotal moment in history. Such reflections made our Moscow home more than just a place to live; it became a bridge to a shared past.

In 1995, Jim Balaschak moved to Russia as managing director to spearhead Teledyne's efforts to expand in the former Soviet Union. After the breakup of Teledyne, he joined Deloitte CIS as chief operating officer in 1998. He repatriated to the United States in 2008. He spent thirteen years on the AmCham Russia board and served as its chairman from 2000 to 2001.

OUR RUSSIAN DAUGHTER
Bhaskar Katta

Our five years in Russia brought many unforgettable experiences, but none more precious than the birth of our daughter, Neha, in Moscow. She is our Russian baby, and her arrival in the heart of winter made the moment even more memorable.

Moscow's winters were both beautiful and unforgiving. I remember my first tentative steps on snow-covered pavements, terrified of slipping on the ice. As an expat unaccustomed to such harsh climates, I struggled but slowly adapted. Another challenge was the language barrier—few in the hospital spoke English, forcing me to learn basic Russian to communicate with the medical staff. It was daunting, but essential during my stay at the perinatal clinic where Neha was born.

Her birth was smooth, but because she was petite—like many Indian newborns—the doctors placed her in an incubator as a precaution. Anxiety gripped me, but within a day, they declared her perfectly healthy and placed her in my arms. The relief was indescribable.

Four days later, we returned home, only to face an unexpected bureaucratic puzzle. With an Indian passport secured, we needed a Russian visa for Neha. But since she hadn't entered the country through immigration, no visa could be issued locally. It was an absurd realization, but with my company's help, we found the only solution—traveling to India, where the Russian Embassy could process it.

At three months old, Neha took her first international journey. Moscow's immigration granted us a strict one-hour window to exit. Once in India, we completed the visa formalities and returned, Neha now officially recognized in the system.

That bureaucratic maze only deepened the meaning of her birth. Moscow became an indelible part of our family's story. No matter where life takes us, Neha will always be our little Russian-born girl—and that memory will stay with us forever.

Bhaskar's international banking career spans seven countries across Europe, the Middle East, Asia, and Australia. He worked with Citigroup during his time in Russia as COO for its Russia and CIS operations (Ukraine and Kazakhstan) and also served for a period as acting CEO of its consumer bank. He currently leads global operations for Australia's second-largest and oldest bank.

LASTING FRIENDSHIPS
Connie Barcenas

I arrived in Moscow on a snowy Sunday morning in February 2005. Jet-lagged but exhilarated, I left my hotel to attend church and buy a winter coat. I wore it the next day—my first at work. After that, I'd rush to my favorite walking spots at the start of snowfall, eager to relive that first morning and watch the Kremlin and Red Square disappear beneath a soft white veil.

I settled into a charming red-brick postwar building on Malaya Bronnaya, overlooking Patriarshiy Prudy. My landlady claimed it was built for Russian generals. The front door lock required three full turns—a minor frustration—but with two vigilant doormen and my landlords nearby, I felt secure in this foreign country where I knew no one and spoke no Russian.

Friendships soon blossomed. Sasha, warm and well-mannered, became my favorite colleague. We bonded over Western music and culture, swapping stories about our families in the U.S. Anya, cultured and curious, was my ever-reliable sightseeing companion. Together, we explored palaces, gardens, and libraries—some off the tourist map—always ending our afternoons with coffee and long conversations.

My landlords were unfailingly kind, always ensuring my comfort. Before my return from a three-week Christmas holiday, they preheated my apartment so I'd step into warmth. My landlady and I, though neither spoke the other's language, conversed for hours—she spoke Italian, I Spanish—bridging the gap with curiosity, gestures, and laughter.

Kolya, my ever-reliable driver, was there in snow, rain, or shine. On my final ride to the airport in July 2007, he handed me two fridge magnets—one of a snow-covered Kremlin, and another of a golden-domed church. Both evoked memories of our drives, when he'd patiently stop every time I wanted to visit a church. Touched, I thanked him.

I also treasure the warmth of my fellow countrywomen in Moscow—Lucille, Eloisa, Carin, Evelyn, Maris, and Maria—whose friendships remain strong two decades later.

My Russian friends welcomed me into their homes, a rare privilege, allowing me glimpses into family life and culture. I often wondered what they thought of me, this dark-haired foreigner with a name that amusingly, matched, that of Vladimir Putin's famous dog, Connie. But despite our differences, we connected as humans, as friends. And I knew they liked our cuisine—after all, they kept requesting it.

I left Moscow with more than memories; I left with friendships that endure.

Connie Barcenas worked for Citibank Russia, based in Moscow, as customer experience head from 2005 to 2007.

MILES TO GO BEFORE WE SLEEP…
John Sartorius

I retired in 2022, but I was fortunate to be in the right place at the right time. Between 1984 and 2011, I lived and worked in Russia for both the U.S. government and private industry—on and off—for nearly half of those years. The people and assignments were wonderful, and there was a great sense of hope and promise as the '80s gave way to the '90s and '00s, with a new generation of young Russian professionals becoming truly integrated into the global community in a way that had seemed impossible in the years before Gorbachev and Yeltsin. In spite of the deteriorating political relationship between the Western world and Russia over the past fifteen years, I draw comfort knowing that life improved for thousands of people because Western companies were there.

While living in Russia, I traveled extensively but almost always for business and on a tight schedule that left little room to see places off the beaten path. I longed for a chance to really see the country, and in 2004, while working on Sakhalin Island supporting oil and gas projects there, I seized the opportunity to take a month-long motorcycle journey with three fellow nutcases. We rode from the Pacific to the Atlantic on the only paved (mostly) road traversing Russia before heading to Ukraine, Hungary, Austria, and points further west.

Among the hundreds of photos, one moment from that trip still resonates deeply: the four of us standing beside our dust-caked motorcycles on the edge of the Urals. We had come thousands of kilometers, and we still had thousands more to go. Sadly, looking at it now reminds me of Dr. Hunter S. Thompson's famous lines from *Fear and Loathing in Las Vegas*: "We had all the momentum; we were riding the crest of a high and beautiful wave. . . . So now, less than five years later, you can go up on a steep hill in Las Vegas and look west, and with the right kind of eyes you can almost see the high-water mark—that place where the wave finally broke and rolled back."

John Sartorius spent most of the 1990s and 2000s living and working in Russia and Kazakhstan. From 1995 to 2000 he was based in Moscow, where he managed the Moscow offices of General Motors and later Hughes Aircraft Systems International and Raytheon Technical Services Company.

ACROSS FRONTIERS
Jeffrey Mankoff

My study-abroad cohort at Moscow State Linguistic University wanted to go somewhere different for spring break. A guidebook described the Altai Republic—where Russia touches Kazakhstan and Mongolia—as a land of stunning scenery and great hiking, not unlike my home state of Colorado.

With little else to go on, five of us booked plane tickets to Barnaul, planning to find someone there who could drive us into the Altai Mountains.

While Moscow in late April called for light jackets, the mountains were buried in snow, with overnight temperatures below zero degrees Fahrenheit. By day, we hiked near the one large road. The birch groves and snow-covered mountains were beautiful, if lacking the grandeur of the Rockies. The bright sun began to melt the snow. By night, we camped in the forest, wrapped in parkas beneath sleeping bags, listening to the wind whip through the trees.

After a couple of days, we were all dirty, exhausted, and increasingly cranky. We took a break at a roadside bus stop when a car pulled up. The driver, a woman of about fifty named Natasha, looked baffled to see five foreign kids in Altai. She took pity on us and invited us to stay with her family in the nearby village of Aya.

Natasha and her husband, Boris (yes—Boris and Natasha), lived with their teenage daughter in a modest home he had built on the banks of the Katun River. Natasha let us sleep in the attic. By day, we took turns going to the *banya* and diving into the frigid river. We hiked with their daughter, who knew the mountains intuitively and outclimbed us all.

Originally from Belarus, Boris and Natasha had moved to Altai after the Chernobyl disaster wreaked havoc on their daughter's health. Natasha taught school; Boris, once an engineer, worked odd jobs and raised sheep, which kept getting stolen. They remained outsiders—natives of one borderland now marooned in a far different one—their Russian village isolated among Turkic-speaking Altais, the region's impoverished indigenous inhabitants.

Boris called his friend Vasily, the local bus driver, who offered to abandon his route for the week and drive us around for $200. We saw petroglyphs and carved pillars dating to the Mongol era and hiked near cairns—each stone, Vasily said, representing a fallen Mongol warrior.

We drank birch sap, dodged ticks, and paddled a glacial lake. Altai felt as far from Moscow as from America: a forgotten frontier—profoundly alien and yet, for a child of the American West, strangely recognizable. What we found in Altai above all was the curiosity and warmth of strangers, despite the mutual incomprehensibility of our experiences.

Jeffrey Mankoff is a scholar and analyst living in Washington, D.C. As an undergraduate, he studied abroad at Moscow State Linguistic University in 1998–99 and returned to Russia frequently until 2020.

SHIFTING PLATES, SOLID CORES
Hans Grisel

It must have been 2011. I was serving a brief stint as an expat in Moscow, wedged between three years in Kyiv and an eventual, if temporary, return to the Netherlands. My career in international banking had taken me across the world, but Russia in those days stood apart—buoyant, confident. Oil and gas were booming, the economy was thriving, and *my* bank found itself at the center of a never-ending stream of truly interesting transactions.

What lingers most from that time, however, are not the deals but two conversations with my second-in-command—a sharp, insightful Russian banker.

The first centered on the surge of shale gas production in the United States. I suggested it might be a game changer, a potential threat to Russia's dominance in the gas industry. He dismissed the idea outright. Russia's geographic proximity to Europe ensured demand for decades, and its rock-bottom production costs would stifle any competition from expensive shale. At the time, his confidence seemed unshakable. And yet, by 2022, it was precisely the rise of shale gas that allowed Europe to sever its dependence on cheap Russian energy. In hindsight, it was the game changer he refused to see.

The second conversation was more philosophical. He drew a striking parallel between Russian and American history—both vast nations whose frontiers expanded by conquest, one moving westward, the other east. He saw in this shared trajectory an explanation for the uncompromising, pioneering mindsets that defined both countries. Though the comparison was simplistic, it was also revelatory. Despite their stark differences, these two rivals bore a deep, almost familial resemblance—nationalist twins shaped by an unyielding sense of destiny.

Now, as I write in 2025, the world order I once knew seems to have unraveled. What comes next is uncertain—the months, even weeks, ahead are a fog of unpredictability. But I suspect those two conversations will remain relevant. The balance of power may shift, the maps may redraw, yet the echoes of the past persist.

Perhaps, like oil and gas, history itself is a resource we mine selectively—ignoring the reservoirs we find inconvenient, convinced that what has always been will always be. Until, inevitably, it isn't.

Hans Grisel is a Dutch banker and worked as country manager for ING in Russia from 2010 to 2011.

LEGAL RECKONING
William Pomeranz

When I lived in Moscow on the eve of the new millennium, I found myself among a generation of ambitious young professionals—lawyers, entrepreneurs, businessmen, journalists, and financial consultants—all wagering, with varying degrees of hope and audacity, that Russia could change. I will never forget the camaraderie of the small, thirty-person law firm where I worked, nor the generosity of my Russian colleagues, who patiently brought me up to speed in a foreign legal world.

I had studied Russian law from a historical perspective—my doctoral dissertation explored the prerevolutionary legal profession, and I had published articles on the nascent constitutional law and early rulings of the Constitutional Court—but I was now stepping into uncharted waters. This was the intricate, high-stakes world of transactional law. And I was doing it in a new language, within a legal system still finding its shape.

So I bought a copy of the Russian Civil Code and the Joint Stock Company Law and set about learning to practice Russian law in earnest, although always under careful supervision. At first, I leaned heavily on my language skills, but slowly the deeper complexities of the Russian legal framework revealed themselves. Everything was new to me, but it was also new for Russia coming out of communism and trying to attract foreign investment. I gradually branched into electronic signatures, contracts, and corporate compliance. It was a great introduction to international and comparative law.

The historian in me could not help but observe, too, the lingering remnants of the Soviet collapse. On street corners, people hawked anything that might fetch a few rubles—tattered books, rusted tools, family heirlooms. Their faces bore the unmistakable imprint of hardship and lives upended.

And then, I witnessed history. On New Year's Eve, 2000, Boris Yeltsin abruptly resigned, ceding power to a little-known figure from the security services. A quarter of a century later, we are still grappling with the consequences of that moment, still asking where Vladimir Putin is leading Russia.

The initial optimism—that Russia might change, might stake its place in the global economic and legal order—has long since faded. What remains is a country beset by economic headwinds: inflation, stagnation, and sanctions. It is a long way from where we imagined ourselves in those heady days after the Soviet Union's collapse. From a personal and professional standpoint, I had an experience of a lifetime—and the memories remain vivid all these years later—but instead of integration, we are once again stuck with a new East-West divide that will take years to overcome.

William Pomeranz is an adjunct assistant professor at the Center for Eurasian, Russian, and East European Studies (CERES) at Georgetown University's Walsh School of Foreign Service. He is an expert on political and economic developments in Russia and Ukraine, particularly as viewed through the lens of law. He is also the author of Law and the Russian State: Russia's Legal Evolution from Peter the Great to Vladimir Putin *(Bloomsbury, 2018).*

CRIME AND PUNISHMENT
Jamison Firestone

It was August 18, 1998. I was 200 kilometers south of Ufa. Russia had defaulted on its debt the day before, but nothing here seemed to have changed. It was six in the morning, and I couldn't sleep. Neither could my client, Phil—a repatriated Russian American with a vision. Phil had imported $20 million in American agricultural equipment, determined to revolutionize Russian farming. We had spent the night at the dreary former collective farm that served as his base.

As we wandered the complex, we noticed a young man, perhaps nineteen, meticulously cleaning the massive wheels of one of the new combine harvesters. The wheels, nearly as tall as he was, didn't need cleaning—they were built for the dirt, destined to roll through it every day.

Phil approached him. "You don't have to clean those," he said gently. "They're designed to work dirty."

The young man turned, gesturing toward the crumbling buildings around him. "Look where I live. Look how we live. My friends drive Russian combines—metal boxes made of scrap that rattle your bones. In the 40-degree sun, they roast in those ovens. My father did too."

He paused, his voice steady but his words charged with pride. "And I sit in this. A glass cabin, air-conditioned, with a chair like a throne that has a shock absorber. There's a stereo and a CD player. I cruise across the fields, music blaring, flying high. Everyone looks at me with admiration, with envy. I feel like a god. And I was nothing. I had nothing. How could I not wake up in the morning and clean this machine?"

Phil's eyes welled with tears.

Phil dedicated himself to transforming lives, to building a better Russia. He built a beautiful estate near Rublyovka for his family—a dream realized, but one that came with a price. One of Vladimir Putin's prime ministers took a liking to the estate and seized it without compensation. Phil was allowed to keep his freedom, but not much else.

Like Phil, I came to understand that those in power did not share our values. They took what they wanted, and the price was paid by those trying to build something better and the people they were trying to help.

Today, Phil lives in America. For similar reasons, I too live abroad.

Jamison Firestone founded the first independent foreign law firm in Russia and lived in Russia from 1991 to 2009.

SERGEI
William Benton Whisenhunt

It was a warm summer day in 1995 when I crossed Senate Square in St. Petersburg and noticed an older man sitting alone on a bench. He wore a blue blazer that seemed out of place in the heat; just watching him made me swelter. As I passed, he didn't seem to notice me at all. I was on my way to the archives in the old Senate building by the Neva, where I briefly placed orders for documents to be microfilmed for my Ph.D. research. I didn't read much in the archives—just ordered thousands of copies to sort through later. This left me time to wander the streets of St. Petersburg, observing people and taking photographs.

On my walk back through Senate Square, he was still on the bench, medals from the Great Patriotic War pinned to his blazer lapel—a common sight among men of his generation. I pretended not to know what they were so I could strike up a conversation. Once I did, he told me his name was Sergei. We spent the next two hours talking about history, Russia, America, and much more—some in English and some in Russian. It was an animated conversation and one of the most enjoyable I've ever had. At one point, he stood up and loomed over me, lecturing about the travesty of how Americans had sent military forces into Russia during the Russian Civil War. He assumed I had never heard of this—but of course I had.

As we wound down our conversation, I asked to take a photograph of him. He agreed. I stepped back, took my 35 mm film camera from my bag, and focused it on him. The image included here is from that day. It remains one of my favorite encounters. He was a delightful, if combative, conversationalist—but in the photo, Sergei appears stoic. Every time I look at it, I smile, remembering the great conversation and what is possible when Russians and Americans speak to each other.

William Benton Whisenhunt is professor emeritus of history at the College of DuPage. His first of ten trips to Russia was in the summer of 1995, when he met Sergei.

THE COUP
David Cant

Moscow, 1991

One August morning—Gorbachev at his retreat in Sochi, me brushing my teeth in Moscow—five officials bring in the military. Glasnost is on the ropes. It's back to the USSR.

In the office, Sasha tells me to leave Moscow.

"No. Let's see what happens."

Day two. The same conversation. My bosses tell me to get out. But I'm getting married here in a week.

That evening, under strict instructions from my fiancée not to leave the apartment, I do exactly that. I walk to the "White House," seat of the Russian Federation. Within forty-eight hours, it has become the frontline for reform.

A man urges support: "Bring tea, blankets, food. Get onto the streets. Show them we are not returning!"

The atmosphere is electric—a coming together, a refusal to return to the past. History is unfolding before me.

Day three. Sasha's face has changed.

"You left it too long. They've closed the airports."

Now I can't leave.

After work, I drive toward central Moscow. Tanks appear suddenly, heading for the Kremlin. They are big, fast—and passing close by my car.

A woman waves a red rose. "Guys, no!" she cries to the soldiers in the tanks.

Time to leave.

I steer closer to a moving tank, cut hard left to slip out the other side before the next tank bears down. As I emerge, a police car flashes by. I narrowly miss being hit. I drive homeward, past Kalininsky—scene of one of the deaths in this coup.

After the U.S. embassy, I can't turn. My progress is halted by a crowd surging toward the Kremlin. My car stops. It's jolted, bumped. I kill the engine, not wanting to antagonize the crowd. A foreigner in a foreign land. I should not be here.

This coup was short-lived. The USSR would soon be dismantled, the genie out of the bottle—for now.

Those charged days in August felt like a turning point—uncertain, but full of hope. People stood before tanks with nothing but flowers and conviction. Strangers brought tea, not just in protest, but out of belief in something better. I remember the sheer audacity of imagining a different future. But now, looking back, I wonder if that moment—so alive, so full of possibility—was the last time Russia stood at the threshold of real change.

David Cant built his career in Russia, where he lived through the tumultuous 1990s before founding his own company and becoming a recognized Russia specialist. A multilingual journalist with a diploma in the field, he has published widely, appeared frequently in broadcast media, and most recently sailed the Atlantic in December 2024—an adventure that ended with his car exploding. He is the author of Unfinished Business: The True Story of a Career with the Russians *(https://amzn.eu/d/dGBJXPM).*

NO REBOUND IN MOSCOW
Bernard Sucher

We must have been watching a game replay that Saturday night, but in the analog world of September 1972, the inconceivable disaster in Munich would not be known until ABC rolled its tape in U.S. prime time. My parents had gone out, leaving me—a twelve-year-old—in charge of my younger brother and sister. Together, in front of our new Zenith color television, we sat in stunned disbelief as the Soviet men's basketball team toppled the United States in the Olympic gold medal game. The scandal of incompetent officiating did nothing to lessen the shame. I broke a lamp in frustration, cried, and—like every patriot—carried the sting of that loss for years.

Two decades later, I was carving out a life in Russia's dilapidated, distressed capital. In a strange land, the stranger may cling to the familiar. My days were consumed by ventures that became a steakhouse, a gym, and the Diner. I worshipped in an Irish pub and fell in with American basketball players. I was the least skilled among them, though tall and strong enough to be of some use.

One bleak winter morning, we trudged across frozen mud to a hulking, dirty white slab opposite Moscow's Gorky Park. We'd paid in advance for the rumor of a gym. That, and the early hour, the biting wind, and our hangovers, testified to our devotion to basketball.

Evidently, others were more devoted still. As we entered through a gloomy tiled hallway, the metallic ring of rim shots and the thwack of dribbles reached us, accompanied by tinny pop music. Inside, a multipurpose room—like an elementary school cafeteria—held flimsy tables, metal chairs, discarded bottles, and food wrappers. Along one wall, men slept amid the debris. In the center, ignoring the remnants of party streamers, eight large men slow-walked a jovial game of hoops.

They were drunk and beaming, but serious when we claimed the court. "This is our place," they said. "You play us, or leave."

One of the sleeping men turned out to be Vladimir Petrovich Kondrashin, coach of the 1972 Soviet Olympic team. It was his birthday, and his surviving players had gathered to celebrate. Though in their forties and coming off an all-night binge, they outmuscled us as if we were children. We couldn't get a rebound and lost by forty points.

Yet it didn't hurt like 1972. Instead, I felt touched with wonder—by human beings who had lived a great and glorious moment. I came to expect such things in my life in Russia.

From 1993 to 2015, Bernard Sucher helped create and lead enterprises in Russia, including capital markets businesses, community and philanthropic organizations, and a range of popular lifestyle establishments.

ONE TOO MANY BLESSINGS
Nora FitzGerald

We arrived in Moscow in the final days of summer 2004—what Russians ominously call the August Curse. When we were driven into the courtyard of Kutuzovsky Prospekt 7/4, my heart did fall slightly. The beige-toned Stalin-era apartment block was in a posh district, across from what was then called the Hotel Ukraine, but it had the look of a place where everything you said might be recorded by a little man in the attic. Turns out this was almost true—but that's another story.

The Kutz was known as the Diplomatic Corpus—aka "foreigner's ghetto"—and the high-alert security guards were hired by the FSB. The drivers who chauffeured the international hires called the speed bump at the entrance the "lying policeman" *(lezhachiy politseyskiy)*. My six-month-old sucked a binky and sat on my lap, while the three older children appeared encouraged by the onion-domed gazebo in the center of the playground and the kids—mostly from Southeast Asia—playing a fierce game of cricket. For a while, that courtyard would be the center of their lives.

We hauled our luggage—and our exhaustion—up to the two-bedroom flat. We collapsed together on the worn sofa. I looked around and felt a flicker of panic begin to rise in my throat.

My first thought at this new home was the expression "one too many blessings." Perhaps saying yes to this posting (did I agree? Who could remember?) was the one too many. I had heard Moscow could be a family graveyard, and some of the experiences of my friends and colleagues were wildly mixed.

And yet others came back changed in a different way. Some returned with stories of improbable friendships, surprising joy, a fierce loyalty to a city that revealed its soul only slowly—if at all.

Then came the month.

In rapid succession, two passenger planes exploded midair—brought down, we were told, by Chechen women: "black widows," the media called them. Days later, a bomb tore through the Moscow Metro. And just as August slipped into September, the siege at Beslan began. More than three hundred dead, many of them children. The country's grief shaped our fear, resilience, and reluctant belonging.

But on that first day, we didn't know any of this yet.

Years later, the memory of that strange old building still lingers—its passing faces, some radiant, some weary. I think often of those who stayed, those who left, and those forever changed.

I was one of them. I miss Moscow, the Russia it could be, and my friends—scattered or still there.

Nora FitzGerald is a writer, editor, and journalist who lived in Moscow from 2004 to 2008, visiting frequently until 2014. For the past decade she has worked in international development.

JUST THE ESSENTIALS
David Jenkins

Day One: May 1995
Arrived at Sheremetyevo Airport in Moscow. The victory lap and leaving party in London are behind me, and a sense of the unknown lies ahead. I'm not afraid—just unaware of what is to come. Excited and tense all at once. I brought only the essentials; "travel light," I was told. I had few belongings in any case, and I have no idea how long this professional and personal adventure will last.

There's a list of sights I must see—Red Square, Lenin's Tomb, St. Basil's, the Old Arbat, and so on. This is Russia, not long after the shelling of the White House—an unstable country beginning to rejoin the international community. What a time to be here.

Russia has a strange reputation back home. I was told to watch out for the mafia and the like—a dangerous place, apparently—but full of promise and intrigue. It's a two-year contract—then I'll likely move on. No long-term plans for now. Time to explore the city. I'm sure there's a good bar around here somewhere—and maybe some like-minded souls.

Day Nine Thousand Eight Hundred: March 2022
The car is fully packed, just the essentials with us. Traveling light is the only option. No victory lap or leaving party this time. No time—or inclination—to celebrate our departure.

For days, my WhatsApp has been buzzing—a strong band of friends from the old Moscow days, concerned for us and asking about our exit plans. Family in the UK is anxious. Russia still has a strange reputation back home.

That was a bit longer than two years. So many close friendships formed since the summer of 1995. I had the opportunity to travel across the entire country for work—yet I still never got to see Lenin's Tomb.

No airport this time. The long road to Tallinn lies ahead. It is, indeed, an escape rather than a departure. I never thought it would come to this.

David Jenkins arrived in Moscow in May 1995 and lived there until March 2022. He built a career in the hospitality and real estate sectors, traveling extensively throughout the country. He has a Russian wife and two children.

THE GRAY MEN ARE GONE
Jeffrey R. Costello

February 1997
Since I'm at the office most nights past midnight, I eat a lot of Jack's—a godsend for expats that delivers pizzas, sandwiches, and actual salads. Russian "salads" tend to be a mystery meat bound to overcooked vegetables with mayonnaise.

Sometimes, walking down the street, I think, *I can't believe I live in Moscow.* The Cold War mystery lingers. I'm finally adjusting to the smell of leaded gas in the air, which reminds me of the 1970s. It also feels like the epicenter of globalization. A financial crisis in Seoul affects London, Moscow, New York, Beijing. Less than six months ago, Moscow wasn't even on my radar. Now it feels inevitable.

There's something radically contingent about Russia right now that appeals to me. It's all the clichés: warm and hostile, brutal and generous, beautiful and ugly, poetic and barbaric. Life isn't terribly hard here—if you have means—but it's no walk in the park for most Russians. Nearly everything is random. Services seem designed to humiliate. Yet people survive through informal, underground networks. There's a palpable sense that history is happening in real time.

The other day, under a crystal-blue sky and arctic sun, I visited the Tretyakov Gallery and "discovered" a painter named Sylvester Shchedrin. In the 1840s, he painted tiny, luminous scenes of Italy—Capri and Sorrento—in a light I've never seen. He must have been from Moscow.

Moscow may be gray and tired, but here and there you find profound beauty. A neighborhood seemingly untouched since the eighteenth century. The lights of the Kremlin after a fresh snowfall. The Cathedral of Christ the Savior is being rebuilt, having been reduced to rubble by Stalin's gray men in the 1930s. They were going to build a tower taller than the Empire State Building. Eventually it became a swimming pool. But the gray men are gone. The city now belongs to the young.

Last Saturday, I went to a little jazz club called Vermeil and met four young Russians—Oleg, Anna, Vlad, and Misha—downing flaming B-52s. They wanted to dance, so we hit Tabula Rasa ("too middle-class," per Anna), then Bulgakov ("too gangster," per Oleg). By 4:00 a.m., I was driving Vlad's car through a blinding snowstorm to Club 011, apparently being the least drunk among us. We danced until dawn, then had champagne and blinis at El Dorado and made plans to do some "real clubbing" next weekend at Titanic.

The gray men are definitely gone—and something magical is happening.

Jeffrey R. Costello completed two stints in Moscow. He was an attorney in the Moscow office of Cleary Gottlieb from 1996 to 1998, then served as general counsel of Brunswick Warburg from 1998 to 1999 and as chief executive officer of Brunswick UBS from 1999 to 2003. He returned to Moscow in 2008 as senior country officer for JPMorgan, a position he held until 2012.

FULL CIRCLE
Alex Geller

February 23, 1980, Leningrad, USSR.
My wife, our three-year-old son, and I walked between two lines of Soviet border guards in green shoulder straps toward the plane that would take us to Vienna and then to the United States. I stopped to wave goodbye to friends who had come to see us off.

"Do not turn your head – голову не поворачивать!" barked one of the guards—just as I remembered my final minutes in the USSR.

Fast-forward to 1995. I sat on a Lufthansa flight bound for St. Petersburg to visit friends and relatives. When the plane touched down, I looked out the window and saw the same border guards, with the same green shoulder straps, who had "seen me off" fifteen years earlier. Suddenly panic seized me. I called the flight attendant and insisted I wasn't leaving the plane—that I was flying back to Munich. It took considerable persuasion before I finally disembarked. And that is how I reentered a country that no longer felt like the one I had fled—or like the one I expected to find.

Over the next twenty-plus years, I spent most of my time in Russia, where I built a successful real-estate development business, completing several well-known projects, including Avon Cosmetics production facilities and Leroy Merlin centers. I joined the AmCham board of directors, created and chaired the Enterprise Development Committee, and championed the value of small- and medium-sized enterprises to young Russian entrepreneurs.

Those years were exhilarating—challenging, often crazy, but always fun. I will never forget one evening when partners from Atlanta, Georgia, arrived in Moscow and I took them to the infamous Night Flight club. Around three a.m., gunshots and screams erupted outside as local gangsters settled a score. My guests panicked, but I maintained a straight face and told them it was a film crew shooting a movie. They relaxed, and we went back to drinking.

Who can forget the Sanduny *banya* (the legendary Сандуны bathhouse)? Or grabbing a greasy burger at Starlite Diner at five a.m. on a Saturday morning after a night of bar hopping?

And then came February 24, 2022. I woke up, checked the news—and my world crumbled.

Within weeks, I shuttered my company, resigned from the AmCham board, left my belongings with a friend, and headed to the airport—heart thudding like it had decades earlier. Once again, I passed beneath the watchful eyes of border guards with the same green shoulder straps. Only this time, I wasn't fleeing the Soviet Union. I was walking away from a Russia I had helped build, now collapsing under the weight of history repeating itself.

Philosopher Xenophon once wrote, "History repeats itself, like a spiral—only on a different level." Lately, I find myself wondering: What level are we on now?

Alex Geller was born and raised in Ukraine. He studied at Tashkent Polytechnic Institute, Leningrad Polytechnic Institute, and LGITMiK (Leningrad State Institute of Theater, Music, and Cinematography). Before moving to the United States in 1980, he was deputy general manager of the Komissarzhevskaya Academic Theater in Leningrad.

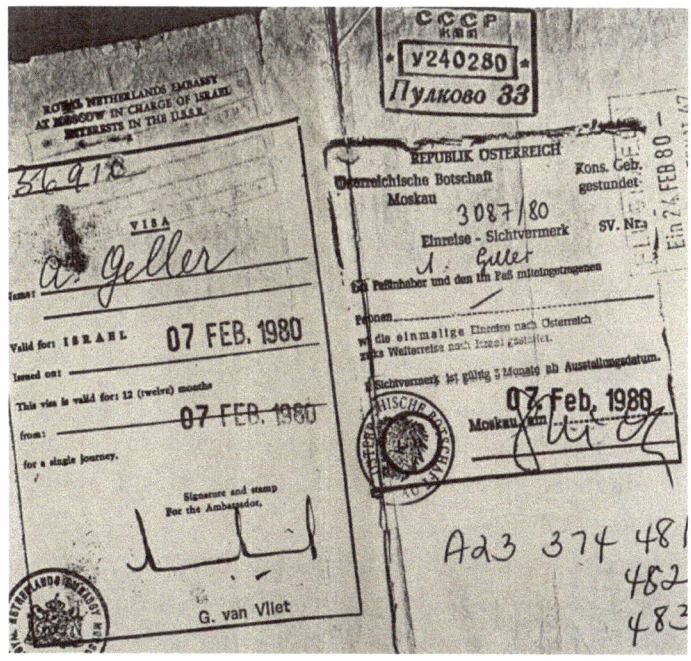

UNLEARNING RUSSIA
Stephen O'Connor

My view of Russia—of the Soviet Union—was shaped in a divided world. It was the enemy: a looming force of control and oppression. My mother, pregnant with me during the Cuban Missile Crisis, remembered the fear that gripped the East Coast. Jacqueline Kennedy reportedly urged the president to accept their fate together if the missiles flew.

The Cold War ran deep in my family. My father was a Marine; his brother was a career intelligence officer; my grandfather fought in three wars. On my mother's side, all her brothers served in World War II, and their sons in Vietnam. Debates over communism and capitalism were family rituals—usually loud, often whiskey-fueled.

My grandmother, Marie Shay O'Connor—born in 1900—was fiercer than anyone. She lived in Seoul from 1946 to 1950 and had many encounters with the Soviet Army. She despised their arrogance and revisionism, clashed with officers at official events, and, family lore claims, routinely used an ice pick to puncture the tires of their Jeeps in protest of their claim to have invented them. She cheered when "those ragamuffins" lost power.

In my twenties, I took a different path—first to Central Europe in the 1990s to support independent media and post-communist economies, then to Moscow in 2007, where I worked in real estate development. I had once feared the Soviet Union without truly understanding it. Now I lived in its former capital and came to know Russians as colleagues, neighbors, and friends.

What I found defied expectations. The years between 1998 and 2014 were, in many ways, the most "normal" Russia had ever known—open, energetic, cautiously hopeful. There was a shared belief among Russians and expats alike that something better could be built. It wasn't perfect—but it was real.

Looking back, I'm grateful for what I unlearned. The rigid certainties of childhood gave way to understanding. The walls I inherited—of fear, ideology, and distance—crumbled within me. Russia is not what I was raised to believe. It is complicated, yes. But it is also human, layered, and deeply alive.

Sometimes I imagine my grandmother meeting my Russian friends. She'd probably scowl, pour a stiff drink, and mutter something unprintable. But I like to think she'd notice what I came to see: that beneath the history and hostility, people are people.

Transformation begins when we do. And healing starts with seeing for ourselves.

Stephen A. O'Connor was the founding publisher of The Budapest Business Journal, The Warsaw Business Journal, *and* The Prague Business Journal *in the years following the fall of the Berlin Wall. He later served as business development director for the Russian real estate joint venture between Lincoln Property Company and AIG. In addition, he was chairman of Big Brothers Big Sisters Russia, among other leadership roles.*

NOTES FROM NOVODEVICHY
Karl Stoltz

"Russia is like radiation," a friend once told me. "Once you've been exposed to it, you'll never get it out of your system."

That may be literally true—I lived in Moscow from 1990 to 1992, when U.S. Embassy Geiger counters once registered alarming spikes at local markets, and again from 2019 to 2021. But I also believe it's true in a more profound, spiritual sense.

Russia lives in me. I carry vivid memories of its culture, people, food, architecture, and daily rhythms—alongside less pleasant recollections of the government's often arbitrary authority and the bureaucratic burdens placed on everyone. Whenever I felt worn down by the latter, I found solace in the former—especially in the quiet refuge of the Novodevichy Convent and its nearby cemetery.

Southwest of the Kremlin and just a reasonable walk from my apartment and the embassy, Novodevichy became a sanctuary across seasons and eras. I walked its grounds in Soviet times, during the chaotic post-Soviet transition, and under the shadow of Putin's consolidated rule. Whether beneath heavy snow, blooming cherry trees, sweltering heat, or golden birches, it was always the same place: reflective, layered, and haunting.

Wandering through Novodevichy's cemetery, I paid my silent respects to Gogol, imagined conversations with Chekhov, and stood reverently before Bulgakov, my favorite Russian writer. I recalled Mayakovsky's fury, Prokofiev's rhythms, Eisenstein's cinematic genius, and Rostropovich's cello. Each path through the cemetery was a promenade through centuries of Russian cultural and intellectual life.

There, too, were the graves of Soviet and post-Soviet leaders I had met in life: Gorbachev, Yeltsin, Primakov, Gaidar. To see their monuments beside Khrushchev or Gromyko was to walk history in reverse, to reencounter those who once shaped the state and now rested among its artists.

My favorite grave belongs to Yuri Nikulin, the beloved clown and actor. Rather than lie in somber repose, he sits on a stone bench, crumpled hat on his head, dog at his side. The memorial is whimsical and poignant—like Nikulin himself, like so much of Moscow life.

Novodevichy is by no means perfect—it, too, has been manipulated by each ruling regime to reflect the propaganda of the day, and is chaotically overcrowded today. But if you love Russian culture, it is the one place you can go in the city to see so much of Moscow's messy, melancholy, and majestic history in the same place. Like radiation, it seeps into you—and leaves you changed.

Karl Stoltz served twice with the U.S. Embassy in Moscow—in the "winds of change" years (1990–92) and in the "frosty climate" years (2019–21). As a U.S. diplomat, he also lived in Denmark, South Africa, Myanmar, Malaysia, Indonesia, Papua New Guinea, and New Zealand, and visited many points in between.

TVER, RUSSIA, 2007
Jason Gresh

Late in the evening, my driver pulled up to the gray, drab apartment block where I would live for the next month. I had arrived in Tver, Russia, at the end of a long day of travel. I had no expectations, but the scene was bleak: an untidy accumulation of trash containers and cars surrounded by a concrete jungle. Exhausted, I followed my hosts, Sergey and Lidia, into a tiny but tidy apartment on one of the upper floors. The contrast with the exterior was striking. Warmth, order, and comfort greeted me.

It was my first time in Russia, part of a language-immersion program after a year of studying Russian at the Defense Language Institute in Monterey, California. I had recently switched my Army specialty from combat arms to become a Foreign Area Officer, focusing on the former Soviet Union. Mastery of the language was the first step.

Tver was mostly gray and cold that time of year—and wet; anything not paved was inevitably muddy. My days were spent at the Tver InterContact Group, taking grammar and conversation classes with a handful of fellow Americans.

Outside the classroom, excursions helped connect the language to the place. Our hosts organized trips to the local theater to see Chekhov and to Lake Seliger and the Nilo-Stolobenskoye Monastery, where time seemed frozen in a sea of birch forest. We even traveled to Mednoe, a memorial to the six thousand Polish soldiers executed by the Soviets in 1940, part of the Katyn massacre. The visit reflected a degree of openness about the past that is rare in Russia today. Access would be difficult now and certainly not included in a program for international visitors.

One often learns the most about a place by talking with its people. Conversations, sometimes awkward, revealed how closely Russians watched the United States—with a mix of fascination, criticism, and an urge for moral equivalency. I hadn't expected how much I would need to listen, and how little I really understood at first.

People often form opinions about a country from first impressions. For me, I came to think of Russia through the lens of Tver—a town of regular people searching for purpose, while grappling with loss. It was here I first met 'patriotic' Russians, prideful but honest people with ingrained views of the West. Yet our interactions were genuine exchanges of views—something rarely achieved in today's acerbic relationship. It is tragic to see where Russia has taken this patriotism today—waging war against Ukraine. I wonder how the war has affected those I met eighteen years ago. I will probably never know.

Jason Gresh is a retired Army colonel who served for most of his career in the spaces of the former Soviet Union. He first visited Russia in 2007 and has continued to engage both professionally and personally with people from Eastern Europe.

NO CRIME, NO PUNISHMENT
Eloisa Klecheski

When my husband was posted to the U.S. Consulate in St. Petersburg in the early 2000s, the city unfolded as a constant delight for our entire family. Among the many things we came to love was learning about Russian literature, and Fyodor Dostoyevsky quickly became one of our household stars. Wandering through the gloomy, timeworn neighborhood where he set *Crime and Punishment* always left us a bit spooked—almost as if Raskolnikov himself might step out from a shadowed doorway—and gave the novel a visceral, lingering weight. We often visited the Dostoyevsky House Museum, located in the corner building where the writer spent the final three years of his life. As was his preference in most of his lodgings, it stood on a street corner and within sight of a church, a detail we began to notice with growing reverence.

The museum sat beside a lively market where we'd shop for groceries—those briny, garlic-spiced pickles remain a fond sensory memory, inseparable from the scent of old books and varnished wood inside the museum. We visited so often that we became friendly with one of the curators, a kind soul who would occasionally slip us small privileges, like letting our children sit on the antique rocking horse once used by Dostoyevsky's own children. It felt like touching a living thread of literary history.

For us, the museum was both tradition and comfort. It became a lens through which we introduced visiting friends to the deeper soul of Russia. Still, our children, then just five, eight, and thirteen, sometimes staged dramatic mini-revolts: "Oh no, not the Dostoyevsky Museum again!" they'd groan with theatrical weariness. But that familiarity—the fact that our children could grow weary of Dostoyevsky—was exactly what charmed our guests. It spoke to the life we had managed to build in this faraway city, one that blurred the lines between the everyday and the extraordinary.

Each visit pressed something deeper into us. I think it was in those quiet, repeated visits—between the squeak of the rocking horse and the cool bite of a winter pickle—that Russia ceased to be foreign. It became a place of memory, meaning, and unexpected joy.

To live in the city where Dostoyevsky set his greatest works was more than a privilege—it gave our time in St. Petersburg a depth and meaning that still echoes.

Eloisa Klecheski lived in St. Petersburg from August 2000 to August 2003, when her husband, Michael, was the political and economic officer at the U.S. Consulate there.

THE CORNER STOP-N-SHOP
Elizabeth Sullivan

It was a dark, bone-chilling February night in 1995, after yet another late evening at the office—my colleagues in New York still struggled to grasp the eight-hour time difference with Moscow. I emerged from Kievskaya metro station to find my neighborhood shop had closed early. The streets were nearly empty, save for a row of elderly women huddled beneath woolen shawls, lining the sidewalk like sentinels of survival. Each one offered a humble spread: a loaf of bread, a package of cheese, or a length of salami.

I moved quickly, selecting enough for a simple dinner, slipping the goods into my string bag—a constant companion in those days—and hurried through the night to my waiting kittens. Purchased on cold winter days, they finally made my Soviet apartment feel like home. They remain the best five dollars I have ever spent.

Months later, on a beautiful June evening—the kind that draws American business travelers to Russia—I hosted my New York-based boss for dinner. As we exited a Metro station, he caught sight of yet another line of women selling food from folding tables and cardboard boxes.

"Who buys food from these women? Who could be so desperate to buy and eat food from the streets?" I looked him straight in the eye and said, "I do. Frequently. When conference calls start at 7:00 pm Moscow time, I don't make it to the shops to buy food. So I'm very grateful to these women selling food, hoping to make a few rubles."

He said nothing. My words lingered in the air.

Of course, the conference call start times remained unchanged.

My boss could not look past the slightly stale loaf of bread to see both the desperation and resilience in these women's eyes. To me, they represented Russia, weary but unyielding, still working and hopeful of a better life even when problems seemed insurmountable. Despite my terrible Russian and foreign awkwardness, they could have been rude to a naïve foreigner like me, but they were always friendly, spoke slowly, and—I'd like to believe—gave me the fresher loaf.

Oddly, I missed their familiar faces when times improved, hoping they were now in warm kitchens, hands wrapped around steaming glasses, gossiping over tea.

Elizabeth Sullivan was with a USAID funded NGO from 1995 to 1997 and with UBS Russia from 1997 to 2013, serving as chief operating officer from 2003 to 2013.

My very "stylish" apartment in 1995, complete with rug and quilt from the Izmailovo Market.

III
EVENTS

In Russia everything is possible, you only have to live long enough.

В России всё возможно, стоит только пожить подольше.

Anton Chekhov, Letter to A.S. Suvorin
Антон Чехов, Письмо к А.С. Суворину
October 27, 1888

RIGHT PLACE, RIGHT TIME: A LIFE SAVED IN MOSCOW
Robert Courtney

It's not every day you have a chance to help save someone's life. For me, that chance came in Moscow on Sunday, October 3, 1993—a day of chaos, violence, and history in the making.

I was ten months into my job as president of the American Medical Centers (AMC), a primary and urgent care clinic created for the wave of corporate expats flooding into post-Soviet Russia. We started in Moscow and later expanded into Ukraine, Poland, Georgia, and Kazakhstan.

That October Sunday, Russia's long-simmering power struggle between President Boris Yeltsin and the parliament erupted. For weeks, parliamentarians had barricaded themselves inside the White House after Yeltsin cut the power. I had assured my visiting father—an experienced ER doctor and trauma surgeon—that things would settle. I was wrong.

By afternoon, the now-armed pro-parliament protesters had stormed across the city and attacked Ostankino, Russia's central television tower, triggering a bloody firefight with government troops. Dozens lay dead, many more wounded. AMC's switchboard lit up with calls for help. Foreigners had been shot and rushed to Sklifosovsky, Moscow's main trauma center. It was time to move.

Sklifosovsky looked like a war zone. A dozen wounded men lay on stretchers in dingy halls, some conscious, others deathly still. Doctors and nurses scrambled between them. Among the wounded was Otto Pohl, a *New York Times* photojournalist, shot through the lung—he was now our responsibility.

Our AMC doctors were general practitioners—very capable, but lacking the trauma expertise we needed. I turned to my father. "Dad, we need you." The Russian doctors took one look at Otto's injuries and asked my father to assist in surgery. Peering over their huddled shoulders, I saw the brutal damage on the scans. The surgery saved Otto's life, but he was in critical condition. Infection risk was high. Keeping him at Sklifosovsky would have been a death sentence.

We arranged for his transfer to Michurinsky Hospital, an elite facility typically reserved for high-ranking government officials. For a week, our doctors worked alongside the Russian medical team to keep Otto infection-free and stable until he could be evacuated to Germany. Two weeks later, he flew home to New York.

The chain of events that saved Otto's life was too precise to be coincidence. Maybe that's just how life works. Or maybe, on that October night, fate refused to let his story end.

Robert Courtney spent more than two decades in Moscow, heading the American Medical Center, founding US Dental Care and several other ventures, and serving on the board of directors of the American Chamber of Commerce.

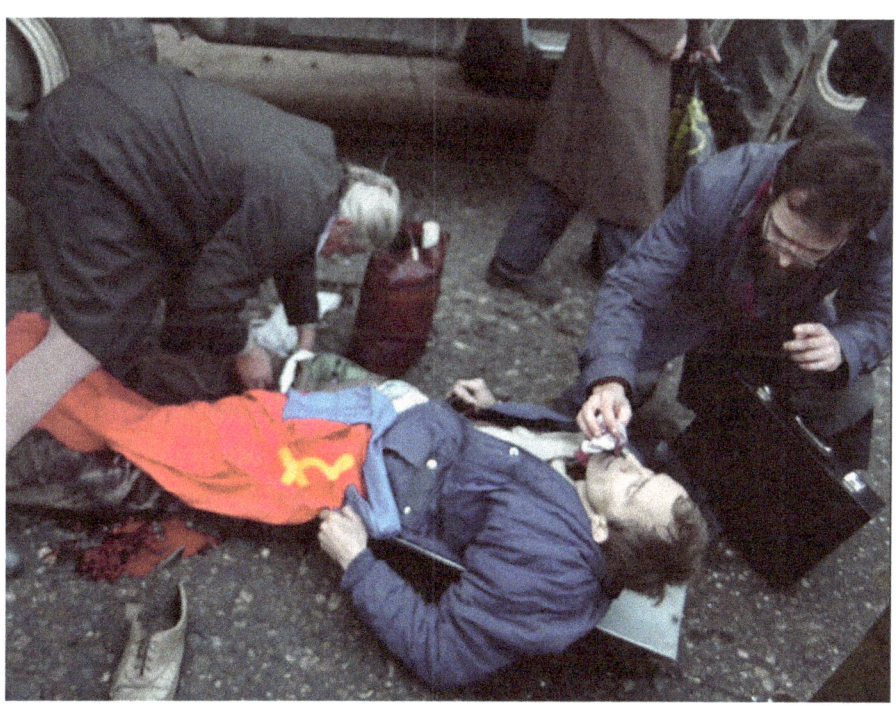

RUSSIA'S LONG ROAD TO TOMORROW
Ben Aris

Russia is famously a country of extremes—revolutions, coups, and bitter winters that turn into blazing summers in days, while snow still lingers in the shadows. There is no coasting in Russia. Nothing is easy. Yet you feel intensely alive there, engaged in a way you rarely are at home—and that is not always a good thing.

I arrived in Moscow in October 1993, at the start of my journalistic career, and walked straight into a crisis that would mark an epoch: President Boris Yeltsin's decision to shell the Russian White House.

Yeltsin was not fully in control. He was locked in a power struggle with a Communist-dominated Duma, led by parliamentary speaker and Chechen professor Ruslan Khasbulatov and Vice President Alexander Rutskoi. They wanted him out.

The reason? The International Monetary Fund had launched its "shock therapy" program, causing economic collapse and plunging an entire generation into visceral poverty.

By September, tensions had escalated. After unconstitutionally dissolving the Duma, Yeltsin tightened a blockade around the White House, where the deputies had barricaded themselves.

On the morning of October 3, Communist supporters marched down Novy Arbat and easily overwhelmed the police. Rutskoi appeared on the White House balcony—an aide holding panels of bulletproof glass before him—and urged the crowd to seize the Ostankino television tower. It was an attempted insurrection. Kalashnikov-toting men poured out of the building, clambered into KAMAZ trucks, and sped away.

Russia's elite Alpha forces reached the tower minutes before the convoy. Then the shooting began.

Crouched behind a tipped-over bus, I heard machine-gun fire crackling from the trees. Tracer rounds lit up the sky in silver arcs. Then came a sharper sound—a *ziiiiip*. Snipers had flanked the bus and begun firing into the crowd. Official reports later said forty-six people were killed that night.

We left the scene. Later at the Bely Tarakan (White Cockroach) bar, rumors were flying: the borders were closed, the government had fallen, the Communists were crushed. No one actually knew what was happening.

In that moment, my sense of the future had collapsed to less than six hours. That's what makes you feel awake in Russia: you never know what the next morning will bring—and it may not be something good.

Ben Aris has been one of the longest-serving foreign journalists, covering Russia since 1993. A former Moscow bureau chief for The Daily Telegraph, *he founded and has managed* bne IntelliNews—*which covers global emerging markets—since 2006.*

COWBOY LAW AT ITS FINEST
John Hewko

My wife, Marga, and I were married in Argentina in December 1989, and two weeks later we moved to Moscow to help open the office of the international law firm Baker McKenzie—the first Western law firm to be officially accredited in the former Soviet Union. I like to joke that Marga was the first, and probably last, Argentine to take a January honeymoon in Moscow. Since no apartments were available through UPDK (Main Administration for Service to the Diplomatic Corps under the Ministry of Foreign Affairs of Russia), home became a room in the Hotel Ukraina, with all the attendant hassles: surly doormen, the infamous floor attendants, or 'key ladies,' and cab drivers who accosted you the moment you left the hotel. Hard-pack Marlboros were the currency of choice. Marga cooked on a hot plate and washed the dishes in the bathtub. A comfortable life it was not.

As a lawyer, however, it was as good as it gets. We were practicing "cowboy law" at its finest, navigating the enormous gap between the Soviet and Western legal systems. Each transaction set a new precedent; laws were changing monthly; and some legislation and regulations were secret. Work was pouring in as our Western clients descended on Moscow. The hours were long and the negotiations difficult—all of which made for an extremely challenging yet exhilarating experience.

Trivial as it may seem, getting a good meal—especially for lunch—was a real challenge. Our office was just off Pushkin Square, and I never thought that one of the culinary highlights of our time in Moscow would be the opening of the first McDonald's. Although the lines during those first months stretched all around the square, it was worth the wait—not just to order a Big Mac, but to soak in the bright lights and Western décor.

It was also a time of incredible political and social change. The protests up and down Gorky Street. The furious and heated debates over the speed and scope of reforms. The Shatalin/Yavlinsky Five Hundred Day Program—intended to transform the country—ultimately contributed to the collapse of the Soviet Union. Yeltsin shocking the 4,500 delegates at the Twenty-Eighth Party Congress by turning in his party card. Each week brought a new twist, a sense that the old world was ending and no one quite knew what would replace it.

It was an extraordinary front-row seat to events that would change the course of history.

John Hewko is a U.S. attorney who practiced law with Baker McKenzie in Moscow, Kyiv, and Prague from 1990 to 2001.

TURKEY IN MOSCOW
Richard Conn

In 1993, Moscow Deputy Mayor Iosif Ordzhonikidze sought advice on attracting foreign capital to the city. He asked me to host a lunch with a few foreign community leaders fluent in Russian. I invited the head of Citibank Russia and the manager of Pat Robertson's telecom venture. The latter gentleman, I'll never forget, accidentally confused *indeyka* (turkey) with *indianka* (Indian) while earnestly assuring a skeptical Russian Supreme Court jurist that "my grandmother was a turkey." He claimed he was one-eighth turkey by blood—a revelation he presented as entirely unremarkable in America's melting pot.

At the time, I was serving as president of the Foreign Bar Association in Moscow. I also advised Gennady Burbulis, Boris Yeltsin's closest aide, on transferring Soviet assets to the nascent Russian state, bringing in Western strategists for Yeltsin's election campaign, and countering Vice President Rutskoi's rebellion. My work was marked by urgency and uncertainty in a nation grappling with profound transformation. Having learned Russian in college, I had persuaded my firm to open its Moscow office in early 1992, inspired by a vague but sincere desire to help build a democratic, free-market Russia.

Our lunch was held at the Anchor restaurant on Tverskaya Street. Seafood was on the menu—mercifully sparing my colleague further turkey-related confusion. On one side sat our small delegation; on the other, Ordzhonikidze and his aides. This was before the deputy mayor survived several assassination attempts, underscoring the volatile environment we were navigating.

Ordzhonikidze began bluntly: "Moscow wants 50 percent of every deal with Westerners."

It became clear he believed the three of us could negotiate on behalf of "the West." I responded diplomatically, suggesting that while profit-sharing with the city was acceptable, we Westerners preferred to do so by paying taxes. Using a colorful soccer analogy, I explained that we saw government as a referee, not a player. I even offered to help Moscow establish a fair tax regime.

To our astonishment, Ordzhonikidze immediately countered, "How about 25 percent?" He thought I was negotiating.

Perhaps my earnestness baffled my cynical host, or perhaps he simply concluded I was, indeed, a turkey.

Surreal ambition, naïveté, and cultural dissonance defined the moment. The stakes were high, the misunderstandings frequent, and the outcome uncertain.

Richard Conn was a partner in the legal firm Latham & Watkins in Moscow.

THE CANDIDATE AND THE BET
William Shor

In early 1996, just out of business school, I landed a job at a bulge-bracket investment bank. My background made me a natural fit for the European Emerging Markets desk: I grew up in a Russian-speaking household—but one that had cheered, loudly, for the collapse of the USSR. That regime had cost us too much.

So when the firm sent me from New York to London and then to Moscow, I believed I was doing more than banking. Like many young idealists, I thought we could help build something better in the post-Soviet world: new markets, new opportunities, a new society.

One of my first real assignments was to accompany a group of top U.S. and European investors on a fact-finding trip to Moscow. These were bold, aggressive fund managers—the kind who saw emerging markets not as minefields but goldmines. We came to gauge the privatization effort and determine whether the door would remain open to Western capital.

The timing couldn't have been worse. Boris Yeltsin, the architect of Russia's economic reforms, was gravely ill and badly trailing in the polls. Gennady Zyuganov, the Communist Party leader, looked likely to win the presidency. A return to state control seemed not just possible but probable.

Moscow that week was grim. The weather matched the mood: leaden skies, thawing streets, people on edge. We met CEOs, bureaucrats, and ordinary citizens, all wondering which way the pendulum would swing.

Then came the meeting that changed the tone of the trip.

Our office arranged for us to meet Zyuganov himself. At the appointed hour, we were led into a grand but faded room. There he was: thickset, gravel-voiced, seated beneath a massive red Lenin banner. He spoke plainly. When he took power, the "good old days" would return. State control would be restored. Privatization would stop.

For a few moments, you could feel the investors calculating their losses—portfolios, careers, entire funds at risk.

But as Zyuganov kept talking, something shifted. He wasn't the ideological zealot of old. He was performing a role, but beneath the surface it was clear: he didn't really want to turn back the clock. What he wanted was to be close to the levers of power—and the rewards that came with that. His message was aggressive, but his tone left space for negotiation. This wasn't revolution; this was haggling.

We left that room with a different view. The risk was real—but so was the opportunity. The market wouldn't vanish. It would simply adjust to a new price of admission.

Many of us returned to our desks and placed trades that reflected that bet: that money—not ideology—would shape Russia's future.

And for a time, we were right.

William Shor earned joint MBA and MIA degrees from Columbia Business School and the School of International and Public Affairs. He began his career at Salomon Brothers and later held senior positions in investment banking, private equity, and venture capital. His work in Russia encompassed proprietary trading, banking, investment structuring, and the organization of one of the country's first large-scale industrial project financings. After nearly twenty-five years in Europe, he now lives in the United States with his wife and children.

VODKA WITH ATTITUDE
Stephen T. Cruty

In 1996, at twenty-seven, I found myself dissatisfied with the grant-driven NGO jobs available to a graduate in international relations and Russian studies from American University in Washington, D.C. The Soviet Union had collapsed, and I was eager for something more adventurous—something on the front lines.

A college friend had landed a job with IBM in Moscow the year before, so I asked to visit and look for work. Upon arrival, I picked up a copy of the *Moscow Business Guide* and went door-to-door to every Western company I could find, asking if they needed Russian-speaking expats. I had no business background—not an accountant, not in sales—but I spoke decent Russian, for an American.

Eventually, someone pointed me toward a British market research firm that needed help writing and translating reports for Western firms trying to navigate this emerging market. That was my foot in the door.

One of our clients was the Seagram Spirits & Wine Group. After two years of "usage and attitude" studies, I casually asked them, "Why are you looking to the past to determine your future?" Russia was waking up. Its future consumers weren't the same ones who had once stood in endless lines for pop-top bottles of Pshenichnaya. They wanted something new, something premium—something with attitude. Seagram hired me to help answer that call.

One of our biggest challenges was introducing tequila to the market. The drink carried cartoonish associations with sombreros and mariachi bands. But some Russians—especially the young—saw past the cliché. They were rejecting the past, reinventing their lifestyles and tastes. Tequila offered something vodka couldn't: energy. We called it "vodka with attitude."

Seagram soon dominated the tequila category with Olmeca and Don Julio. We created a cocktail culture driven by bold flavors and nighttime promotions that ran from midnight to dawn in Moscow's wildest clubs. Sometimes we came straight from the bar to the office—but we were building something: a brand, a culture, a sense of freedom.

For many expats, Russia in the 1990s felt like a half-built stage, the scenery still shifting, the script unwritten—and it made one feel undeniably alive. Reflecting on the brushes we survived with the mafia (and our *krysha*, or protective "roof"), the GAI, the KGB, the OMON, the babushkas who scolded you on the Metro for daring to go hatless in winter, and the ranks of profit-driven *dyevs* (girls) is enough to make any parent shudder. And yet, for this young American, those years passed like a fever dream—equal parts chaos and clarity, always pulsing with the sense that anything could happen, and often did.

Stephen T. Cruty studied in Russia at Moscow State Linguistic University in 1991 and at the Moscow State University School of Journalism in 1993. He returned to Moscow in 1996, working for the Russian Market Research Company and the Seagram Spirits & Wine Group–Europe. His tenure in Moscow concluded in 2002, following Seagram's sale and departure from the Russian market.

A TALE OF CRISIS, CURRENCY, AND COUTURE
Peter Westin

I arrived in Moscow in July 1998, ready to take on my new role at an EU-funded think tank as an economic advisor to the Russian government. After settling into my apartment in Chisty Prudy, my first major excursion was to the Kremlin. After a stroll around Red Square and St. Basil's Cathedral, I ventured into a new underground shopping mall, swarming with the *nouveaux riches*.

Amid the luxury goods, one item immediately caught my eye: a brown leather coat. I tried it on, and not only did it fit perfectly—it seemed to have my name on it. But upon closer inspection, it read "Versace," and the price tag was a whopping $8,000. My dream of owning haute couture deflated faster than a balloon at a four-year-old's birthday party. I left empty-handed.

A month later, disaster struck: Russia defaulted on its external debt, sending the ruble into a downward spiral. As an economist, it was morbidly fascinating to watch. While the news was full of doom and gloom, there was an eerie sense of calm on the streets of Moscow. People lined up outside banks to withdraw their rubles, but Russia had been dollarized for nearly a decade. Many had already exchanged rubles for dollars, serving as a natural hedge as the ruble lost value. By then, the ruble money supply was only 14 percent of GDP.

However, the financial system was in tatters. Bankruptcies soared, and retailers, facing a liquidity crunch, were slashing prices to stay afloat. A week after Russia's default, I returned to the same shopping mall. The atmosphere had changed: the crowds were gone, and everything was on sale. And there was my brown leather coat. I checked the price tag: $800. I couldn't pass it up.

At checkout, I faced a "cash only" sign, all ATMs conveniently out of order, and I didn't carry that much cash. After pleading in broken Russian, the manager agreed to accept my credit card. He swiped it with a ZipZap machine, and I walked away, coat in hand.

The coat now rests in my closet, a relic of a country that no longer exists in the way I remembered it. I spent fifteen years in Russia, each year stitched with its own complications, absurdities, and quiet revelations. But the coat? It rarely leaves its hanger. Perhaps it belongs more to the memory than to the man. Or perhaps it was never really mine—but Russia's sly gift, offered at a moment when history forgot to check the balance.

Peter Westin, PhD, is the executive director of the Arditti Risk Management Center at DePaul University, where he also teaches finance. An active angel investor, he spent fifteen years in Russia, serving as chief economist and chief equity strategist at JPMorgan and at various investment boutiques. He has coauthored two books on Russia.

LOST IN TRANSITION
Dominique Menu

On September 16, 1991, I boarded AF270 to Moscow to assume my new role as head of the representative office. Over the previous two years, I had worked on two major Soviet projects: establishing a leasing company in East Berlin to finance transportation equipment for Soviet-owned Western subsidiaries, and structuring the financing for Aeroflot's first Airbus purchase.

For the leasing project, I reminded my superiors that, under the Soviet constitution, all capital goods belonged to the state. However, Soviet-controlled companies based in the West offered a legal workaround. My 1979 dissertation on Soviet banks had given me confidence in navigating these structures.

The Aeroflot deal was equally complex. We enlisted a Soviet law professor to propose a constitutional amendment allowing aircraft leasing. When Aeroflot's CFO suggested a Japanese tax lease, I pointed out a geopolitical obstacle: the Soviet seizure of the Kuril Islands in 1945 meant that Japan and the Soviet Union had never signed a peace treaty, making such an arrangement impossible.

As we flew over Poland, the plane suddenly looped back. When I questioned a stewardess, she dismissed my concern—until I pointed out the shifting sun. After checking with the cockpit, she admitted we were ahead of schedule, and lacked Soviet airspace clearance. Rather than risk a confrontation with Soviet air defenses, the pilot wisely circled until given permission to enter.

In Moscow, after the customary handover, I traveled to St. Petersburg for meetings with Mayor Anatoly Sobchak. Our partner, Dresdner Bank, aimed to open a branch and reclaim the former German embassy as its headquarters. They hired Matthias Warnig, a former Stasi officer with ties to Vladimir Putin—then serving as head of the Committee for External Relations in the mayor's office—to manage negotiations.

Back in Moscow, I attended the first gathering of independent Russian bankers at the Cosmos Hotel. Many resisted disclosing financial data to

Gosbank, and I reassured them that such reporting was standard in the West.

I also met with Russia's newly established Central Bank, then competing with Gosbank. Governor Georgy Matiukhin, who spoke fluent French, greeted me warmly and, with a sly smile, explained that we could follow either institution's regulations—or neither.

As the Soviet Union teetered on collapse, I barely secured my exit visa. On December 21, I flew home to Paris, arriving just in time to watch Mikhail Gorbachev resign. A new era had begun.

Dominique Menu first visited the Soviet Union with his high school in 1973 and 1975. He served as head of the representative office of Banque Nationale de Paris for the Soviet Union and Russia in Moscow from September 1991 to October 1994.

RUSSIA AND THE EUROPEAN APPROACH
Seppo Remes

I was the founder of the Association of European Businesses (AEB) and, from 1995, served as its chairman.

The AEB brought together businesses from all EU member states. It was not only a networking platform but also a forum for informing members, arranging contacts with the government, and lobbying for improvements in the business environment—particularly for EU companies. We had committees organized by industry and by function, such as taxation and customs. Government officials and business leaders were regularly invited to speak at member meetings. Once a month, we held a "EuroDrinks" event at an EU country's embassy—an informal but valued tradition.

One afternoon, I received a call from the deputy prime minister's office. The next evening's EuroDrinks was to be held at the Finnish Embassy. The Russian deputy prime minister, Viktor Khristenko—whom I knew from the Energy Dialogue and who was responsible for EU economic relations—wanted to attend. He also wanted to bring Russian journalists.

Technically, I could not authorize his participation—it was the ambassador's event. And personally, I hesitated. We had a firm principle to keep EuroDrinks internal. I was uneasy about making it public. I shared my concerns with Khristenko's office. A few hours later, they called back and gently pressed me to agree. During the call, I had an idea: perhaps we could use the opportunity to announce something positive for the business community. They liked the idea, but time was short.

I proposed that we announce, at a press conference, a new initiative: monthly meetings between the AEB and the deputy prime minister, held at the Russian government building—the White House. It was quickly agreed.

The initiative became reality and lasted for about a year. It was a time when the Russian government showed genuine interest in closer ties with Europe, particularly in economic and energy affairs. The atmosphere was open and constructive. The AEB compiled lists of issues and proposals, which were discussed directly with Khristenko—a rational, forward-looking figure. Driving to the White House each month without ceremony felt like a small but meaningful success.

Eventually, though, the AEB could not maintain the needed depth of preparation, and the momentum faded. The Russian government's mood also shifted—from dynamic European outreach to more routine engagement.

Looking back, it was a window into a very different Russia—a time of possibility, when dialogue felt sincere and progress seemed within reach. Those were good days, and they are deeply missed.

Seppo Remes worked for twenty-two consecutive years in Moscow, from 1993 to 2015—first as the local head of the Finnish oil and gas company Neste, which later merged with the power company Fortum. He subsequently served as an independent director on the boards of several major Russian public companies, including UES, Sibur Holding, Rusnano, Rosseti, Sollers, and OMZ.

SATURDAY WITH THE GOVERNOR
Eugene Belin

My country manager called me on a Friday evening in October 2008. "Eugene, we need to meet the governor of the Central Bank of Russia at 10 a.m. tomorrow."

"Saturday?"

"That's right. All major foreign banks in Russia have been summoned."

At the time, I was head of financial markets and country treasurer of Citibank Russia, a subsidiary of Citibank New York, the most globally connected U.S. bank. Since its 1993 return, Citibank Russia had expanded rapidly, mirroring the country's booming economy and financial sector. By 2008, we were a major player, serving both international corporations and Russia's largest companies, with consumer branches across major cities and over a million Russian clients.

By that weekend, the global financial crisis had reached full intensity following Lehman Brothers' collapse in September. The Russian ruble was in free fall, and everyone clamored for U.S. dollars, the ultimate safe haven. Our balance sheet swelled as individuals and corporations rushed to exchange rubles for dollars and deposit them in foreign banks, perceived as safer than Russian institutions. Cautious by nature, we placed these funds with our New York parent and in U.S. Treasuries—assets we deemed the safest.

That Saturday, we sat across from the Central Bank governor and his head of markets in a grand meeting room. Generally regarded as a competent institution, the CBR welcomed foreign banks, believing they elevated industry standards and improved services. We had strong relationships with many officials, including the head of markets. But this time, the mood was icy.

They demanded we repatriate the offshore U.S. dollar deposits, fearing that if capital controls were imposed, these funds would become inaccessible, jeopardizing Citi Russia's liquidity. As our lead regulator, they left us no choice. Our protests—that this influx of deposits was involuntary and driven by Russian clients—were dismissed outright.

What to do? Depositing dollars with Russian commercial banks was out of the question, and the CBR offered no U.S. dollar deposit facility. The only viable option was purchasing Russian government dollar-denominated bonds.

Convincing Citi's risk managers in New York and global markets leadership in London was no small feat. Eventually, we prevailed, acquired the bonds, and as the crisis eased, reaped significant profits.

One of many vivid chapters from my professional life in Russia, where the pulse of opportunity once beat strong. Before relations with the West frayed, it was a land of dynamism, risk, and reward—an exhilarating, often lucrative arena. Yet beyond the balance sheets and boardrooms, I most cherish the brilliant, diligent, and warmhearted Russian colleagues who infused every challenge with resilience and camaraderie, leaving an indelible mark on both my career and my memories.

Eugene Belin covered financial markets with Citibank and Deutsche Bank, including a decade in Russia (2001–11) as Citibank's head of markets for Russia, the CIS, Israel, and Eastern Europe. He served as a board director of Citibank Russia and as chairman of the board of Citibank Kazakhstan (2017–21).

MOSCOW MEMORIES
Steve Ridlington

Having spent forty-four years working across seven countries, I can say with certainty that my years in Russia were the most exhilarating. Nowhere else did I encounter such extremes of drama and unpredictability. Moscow offered a cultural immersion unlike any other, but beyond that, it was a place where the unexpected lurked behind every ordinary day—a single red rose auctioned for $5,000 in a restaurant, or the surreal realization that the Moscow Big Bus tour's first stop was my own apartment complex.

Not all surprises were so benign. One crisp spring morning, I arrived at the office, unaware that by nightfall I would be the last employee left in the building—held incommunicado under the watch of the FSB.

The raid began midmorning. A swarm of young men in jeans, T-shirts, and baseball caps flooded in, their casual dress belying the authority they wielded. I was confined to my office, forbidden from making calls. I knew the combination to one safe—mine. The other had belonged to my predecessor. I was instructed to open both safes. I opened my own but explained that I could not open the other.

Tension thickened. Officers conferred in hushed but urgent tones. What was inside? How would they open it? I had no answers. As the hours dragged on, colleagues were gradually dismissed until I alone remained. Evening deepened. No food, no word to my wife, no idea when—or how—this would end.

Then the senior officer's eyes landed on the golf set in the corner of my office. With a silent gesture, he asked if I played. I mimed a response. In an instant, we understood each other.

The corridor filled as his subordinates gathered to watch. He putted—cheers erupted. I putted—boos followed. The game was no contest, but it didn't matter. The mood had shifted. Laughter replaced the oppressive silence and, as if summoned by fate, the safebreaker finally arrived.

Minutes later, the safe was open, its mystery resolved. I was free to go. As I left, I shook hands with men I had never met and would never see again.

Only in Russia could a day that began with a raid end with a round of golf.

Steve Ridlington has served as TAQA's chief financial officer since July 2020. Previously, he was chief investment officer at Abu Dhabi Power Corporation. He also held positions with the UK Ministry of Finance, BP, TNK-BP, and the National Central Cooling Company PJSC (Tabreed), where he served as CFO. He holds a Master of Philosophy in economics from St Antony's College, Oxford, and a Bachelor of Science in economics and mathematics from the University of Sussex.

FOR THE LOVE OF IZMAILOVO
Constance McCaslin

Times of cultural upheaval often create immense opportunity—but rarely without chaos. For foreigners witnessing post-Soviet Russia, few places captured this upheaval like the flea market at Izmailovsky Park, known simply as Izmailovo.

Poets, professors, and physicians—many made redundant by collapsing Soviet institutions—manned the stalls, selling everything from folk art to family heirlooms. The *matryoshkas*, amber jewelry, and lacquer boxes came with stories of personal survival, lost ideologies, and unexpected renewal. Ask about a lacquer box, and you might get a history of icon painters reinventing themselves after the fall of Imperial Russia. A discarded oil painting might lead to a conversation about Constructivism, the Bauhaus, or a vendor's own artistic struggle.

While luxury boutiques opened downtown, my friends and I preferred the snow-dusted paths of Izmailovo, where we found apothecary bottles etched in Cyrillic, antique inkwells, and postcards from Soviet holidays past. A new entrepreneurial spirit surfaced in *matryoshkas* featuring Harry Potter or Soviet leaders in sports gear.

One expat woman became an expert in glass New Year's ornaments. Since religion had been suppressed, Russians marked the New Year with trees and whimsical, secular decorations. Her collection, gathered over years, was profiled in a Russian magazine. Soon after, it was declared a cultural treasure—"donated" to remain in Russia permanently.

Another friend returned from the market concealing a very ordinary-looking rock. "It's a meteor," she confessed. The vendor explained that his father had collected the fragments after a 1970s Siberian fall. She believed him.

The market grew. Samovars gleamed, *shashlik* sizzled, and shoppers warmed themselves beside grills in temperatures that often dipped to minus twenty. I visited most weekends during my seven years in Moscow.

On a bitterly cold day, my visiting mother and I encountered a pack of Izmailovo's infamous wild dogs. One lunged and bit deep into my thigh, then noiselessly walked away. I felt the blood running but, not wanting to alarm my mother, calmly told her I knew where to find first aid.

Well, not exactly a first-aid station—but the woman I knew who monitored the outdoor toilets had water and disinfectant for paying customers. She cleaned my leg, slathering it with some kind of orange disinfectant that looked a lot like the mercurochrome of my youth. As she wrapped the wound, she muttered, "They bit a child yesterday."

The next weekend, I returned to thank her. "Where are the dogs?" I asked.

"We shot them," she said matter-of-factly.

I guess the dogs were just the latest victims of the harsh realities of this new regime.

Constance McCaslin lived in Moscow for seven years with her husband, who worked at the U.S. Embassy, and their three sons.

RIDING RUSSIAN RAILWAYS
Scott Gehlbach

I spent four to five years of my adult life in Russia. Beginning in 1998 and for many years thereafter, I lived part of each summer in St. Petersburg, where my wife was born and her family still resides. From 2001 to 2003, I wrote my dissertation at the New Economic School (NES) in Moscow. From 2007 to 2008, I returned to NES as a Fulbright-Hays Fellow. Among my happiest memories from those years are the long train rides I took within Russia.

The Russian economy fluctuated during this period, and the government slid steadily into unrepentant authoritarianism, but the trains kept getting better. I recall an early ride in *platskart* (budget class), sitting in the dark at the station—lights off to conserve battery power—waiting to depart. Only once the train began to move could passengers see well enough to arrange their things. Yet even then, the trains ran on schedule. "Bang on time," I remember a Lonely Planet guide noting. As new money flowed in and rolling stock was upgraded, rail travel became reliably comfortable.

Trains were places of conversation, and I had many over the years. On a journey to Saratov, I sat in the dining car with Konstantin Sonin—a prominent Russian economist and now my colleague at the University of Chicago—and sketched out an early game-theoretic model of "Bayesian persuasion." On another trip, I spoke late into the night with a Russian naval officer based in St. Petersburg. I've occasionally wondered if he felt compelled to report our exchange.

Every train ride ends. If one is lucky, the conversation continues after disembarking. For the truly fortunate, it continues over *kalitki* (open-faced pies) and tea, as it did when I traveled with my wife's family to the Karelian village where my mother-in-law was born. I've eaten at fine restaurants, but no other meal was quite so satisfying.

Eventually, I graduated to *kupe* (compartment class), with a locking door and a bed long enough for my feet. It was an upgrade—but with higher stakes. On that same Saratov trip, Konstantin negotiated a cabin change after I complained about the unbearable body odor of two men sharing our space. "How did you manage that?" I asked. He smiled: "Foreigners are a little bit boss, a little bit child."

That last memory is bittersweet. Gone are the days when I could be indulged for my oddities. Today, soldiers ride those same rails—to kill, and to be killed. But I recently boarded a Soviet-era car traveling between Poland and Kyiv. The conversation was excellent, the ride smooth, the journey complete.

Scott Gehlbach is the Elise and Jack Lipsey Professor of Political Science and Public Policy at the University of Chicago. Throughout the 2000s and 2010s, he was affiliated at various times with both the New Economic School—twice as a Fulbright–Hays Fellow—and the Higher School of Economics in Moscow.

STITCHES
Brian D. Taylor

Our twin sons, Anatol and Lucian, were nine when we moved to St. Petersburg. My wife, Renée, and I were teaching as Fulbright Scholars at the European University at Saint Petersburg.

We arrived in January 2011, when St. Petersburg is glorious but cold and dark. All winter, we warned our sons against horseplay. "Be careful," we admonished. "You don't want to go to a Russian hospital."

Jinxed.

That July, we traveled to Altai, near Russia's border with China, Kazakhstan, and Mongolia, to visit friends who had a dacha in Manzherok on the Katun River. A beautiful place—serene and wild.

One afternoon in the woods, Anatol slipped on pinecones and fell onto a sharp rock. The cut was straight but deep, and blood trickled down his leg. He needed stitches. Renée made a makeshift tourniquet to stanch the bleeding. We jumped into the car—Renée, our host Vanya, and I—and set off to find the village doctor.

She was working in her garden, wearing surgical gloves. She said regretfully that she lacked the necessary supplies and sent us to a small urgent care clinic in a nearby town.

It was Friday afternoon, and the main clientele at the clinic seemed to be people who had injured themselves while drunk. The head doctor angrily explained they lacked proper supplies for stitches. Back to the car—and on to the children's hospital in Gorno-Altaysk, the regional capital.

What we encountered was a world apart from any U.S. hospital. No intake forms, no ID checks—no questions at all. Within minutes, Anatol was in an exam room. A nurse told everyone to leave. But Anatol was nine, in pain, afraid, and understood no Russian. I grabbed his hand and refused to go.

The doctor worked quickly, using just two stitches—where in the U.S., six or seven would have been the norm. But it did the trick.

Fifteen minutes later, we were walking out. No bill, no post-op instructions.

Back in St. Petersburg, we paid $100 at the European Medical Center to remove those same two stitches. A stark contrast to Gorno-Altaysk.

Vanya insisted that Anatol learn the phrase *U menya dva shva*—"I have two stitches." Years later, it remains one of the few Russian phrases he remembers.

Brian D. Taylor first visited the Soviet Union in 1985 and traveled to Russia many times for his academic work between 1990 and 2019. He was a Fulbright Scholar in St. Petersburg in 2011.

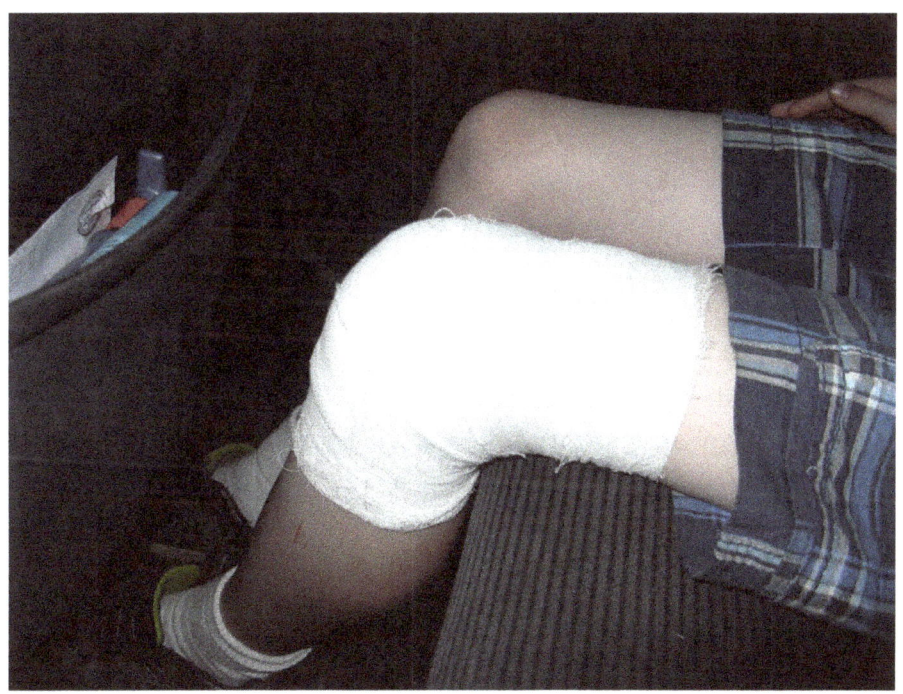

ROMANOVS, BOLSHEVIKS, COMMUNISTS
Patricia E. Dowden

Many years ago, when many of us were fascinated by meeting such interesting Russian friends and looking forward to cooperation in creating a new future for Russia, I attended a dinner hosted by Arden House (an academic initiative of Harvard and Columbia) and was seated next to one of the speakers—a senior executive with a Western company's Russian subsidiary. We found a topic of mutual interest: the legendary House on the Embankment.

I told him about my visits there as a B&B guest of the granddaughter of Yakov Sverdlov. Sverdlov was Lenin's right-hand man before Stalin; he died in 1919 in the Spanish flu pandemic. One rumor suggests that his widow had been given custody of the Romanov jewels taken after their execution—the getaway funding in case the Bolshevik Revolution failed. She was given a top-floor apartment when the House on the Embankment was built; it was still occupied by her grandchildren. I'm guessing it hadn't changed much in the intervening years—lots of dark red velvet, a very lumpy bed, and family photos above the bed of Sverdlov's family and colleagues—Lenin, the St. Petersburg revolutionaries.

The granddaughter (my hostess) was a university professor; her husband was a diplomat to the U.S.; and the grandson, unemployed, was sometimes my driver. She told wonderful family stories and had boxes of letters, including love letters, that she was about to donate to the Russian archives. She swore her grandfather had no role in the Romanov execution.

My dinner companion told me his family had also lived there.

"So," I said, "your family was part of the Soviet government?"

"Yes, my great-grandfather was president of Russia!"

I took another look at his name tag: **Alexander Mikoyan.**

He told me that his mother had been the researcher for a recently published book, *Michael and Natasha: The Life and Love of Michael II, the Last of the Romanov Tsars*. By chance, I had already found it in the Heathrow bookshop—a fascinating and tragic story. Ironically, his mother—a

Bolshevik revolutionary's granddaughter—was granted access by Moscow State University's philology department to the intimate correspondence of Grand Duke Mikhail and his wife Natasha, chronicling their love story and final days. She even found the telegram signed by Yakov Sverdlov ordering the execution of the Romanov family.

And the ironies continue: in 2006, Alexander Mikoyan represented a bridge between Russia's troubled past and future in cooperation with the West. Today, he lives in self-imposed exile in London.

Patricia Dowden's Russia career began with an Alfa Bank consultancy in 1997. She lectured on management in Russia's regions, worked with large companies on an ethics self-evaluation system, and collaborated on ten business ethics conferences with St. Petersburg State University of Economics and the Wharton School.

(Left to Right: Grand Duke Mikhail Alexandrovich,
Yakov Sverdlov, Anastas Mikoyan)

IV

ABSURDITY

Everything that's happening is absurd.
There's no way to escape it, and even if you try, it's already too late.

Все, что происходит - абсурд.
Из этого нельзя выйти, и даже если
ты попробуешь, уже поздно.

Sergey Dovlatov, The Suitcase
Сергей Довлатов, Чемодан
1986

1996, GROZNY, REPUBLIC OF CHECHNYA, RUSSIA
T. Hawk Sunshine

I leaned my elbows on the table, which wobbled precariously. The cup of steaming tea before my bearded host slid ominously toward the edge.

In my mind's eye, I watched it happen in slow motion—the cup tipping, scalding liquid spilling onto his crotch. He'd shriek, leap to his feet, and one of his heavily armed guards would promptly shoot me in the face.

My host was Shamil Basayev, the most infamous Chechen terrorist in Russian history.

The day before, I had met with the commandant of Grozny, intent on piecing together how the Chechens had managed to seize the city from a vastly larger Russian force. The official story was murky and contradictory. I offhandedly asked if a meeting with Basayev was possible. The commandant was noncommittal: "Come back tomorrow at 8 a.m.," he said.

At the appointed hour, two guards with AK-47s led us from the commandant's headquarters through a deserted park along a cement wall. Perhaps my casual interrogation of the commandant's inconsistencies had irritated him. Chechens have a well-earned reputation for handling insults with "efficiency." The setup had all the charm of a Stalin-era punishment—lined against a wall, shot in the back of the head.

I slowed my pace, putting distance between myself and the others . . . maybe I'd have a chance to scale the wall while my colleagues were executed. One of them caught on and did the same. Solidarity.

We reached a lone apartment building and were told to wait outside with the guard while our escorts entered the building. The guard looked like he'd been assembled from spare parts—his face a roadmap of scars, a wickedly curved knife jutting from his belt. Would we be shot in the basement?

The wait was excruciating. The uncertainty, worse. I forced a smile and told the guard his knife was cool. He grinned—a full, toothy display—and to my surprise, unsheathed it and handed it to me. That seemed like a good sign.

At last, our escorts reappeared and led us upstairs. In a top-floor apartment, Basayev sat among fighters bristling with weaponry. He motioned us toward the kitchen, where hot tea, cheese, and bread were laid out.

It appeared the execution was off. For now. I had come seeking answers; instead, I left with a knife, a memory, and the unsettling sense that survival often hinged on little more than luck.

T. Hawk Sunshine is a former investment banker, U.S. Army officer, and entrepreneur based in the United States. He earned his PhD from the University of the Russian Ministry of Foreign Affairs (MGIMO).

TIR
Laura Brank

I arrived in Moscow in the summer of 1995. I had visited before, but only briefly; this time, I was moving there to live and work. The difference was profound. Expats had a phrase to explain Moscow's quirks and contradictions—the everyday absurdities of Russian life.

"What in the world was that?" a newcomer might ask, only to receive a knowing shrug and the terse reply: "TIR"—short for *This Is Russia*.

Russians, I soon found, could be warm and funny one moment, stone-cold and impenetrable the next. But one trait remained constant: a stoic fatalism. This was never clearer than on one February night when I was flying back to Moscow with two Russian colleagues after a business trip to Tatarstan.

The flight had been turbulent from the start, but when our aging Tupolev suddenly plunged in a sickening free fall, my stomach followed. No announcement came from the cockpit. The plane continued to lurch—loose luggage tumbling from overhead bins, paper-thin seats flopping forward and back. Russian flight regulations, it seemed, had little concern for securing such things. Also unsecured was an odd assortment of dirty oxygen masks that suddenly dropped in front of us. Again, no announcement from the flight deck.

Without warning, the nose dipped sharply. There was no noticeable reduction in speed, but the direction had changed dramatically. We were landing—at full speed, with no extended flaps to slow our descent. I glanced at my colleagues. Their eyes, wide as saucers, were fixed ahead, unreadable. Then, miraculously, the plane steadied just seconds before slamming onto the tarmac in a bone-rattling bounce.

Unfortunately, we had landed at the wrong airport—far from the cars waiting for us. Any explanation from the flight crew? None. Once the plane rolled to a halt, the flight crew emerged from the cockpit, casually strolling down the aisle to the enthusiastic applause of the still-seated and very pale passengers. It was the local custom for passengers to remain seated and wait for the crew to exit the aircraft first.

I turned to my colleagues. "That was the scariest flight of my life."
They shrugged. "We need to get in line to call for a car."
TIR.

Laura M. Brank is a partner at the international law firm Dechert LLP. She became the managing partner of Chadbourne & Parke LLP's Moscow office in August 1998—just before the Russian government's default on its domestic debt and the massive devaluation of the ruble—and remained in Russia, on and off, for the next twenty years.

THE ART OF MOTION
Steven Thunem

When we arrived in Russia in 2001, we expected cultural surprises, linguistic challenges, and bureaucratic puzzles. What we did not anticipate was that simply getting from one place to another would become an adventure in its own right. Driving in Russia—or rather, the uniquely fluid interpretation of traffic rules—was one of the country's most curious and exhilarating spectacles.

The very concept of a two-lane highway was more of a polite suggestion than a binding regulation. In moments of congestion, a two-lane road could swell to accommodate four, five, even six lanes of vehicles—drivers maneuvering with an almost balletic disregard for painted lines. The opposing lane? Fair game for those in sufficiently large black sedans, especially if they bore the ominous flashing blue lights of bureaucratic privilege. And then there were the railway tracks—an alternative, if perilous, route for those seeking to bypass the paralytic snarl of city traffic.

Speed limits existed, but only as distant echoes of an idea. I recall one particularly exhilarating return from the airport, my vehicle hurtling along the highway at a dizzying 220 kilometers per hour—a pace that might have seemed suicidal elsewhere but was, in the context of Russian roads, merely ambitious.

Yet for all this glorious anarchy, a curious order reigned. Enforcement ebbed and flowed, dictated less by legal statutes than by the rhythms of the calendar. As holidays approached, the watchful eye of the traffic police grew noticeably sharper—their motivation not rooted in civic duty, but in the simple reality that official salaries were meager and festive celebrations required additional funds.

It was during one such pre-holiday crackdown that I found myself pulled over. A routine U-turn—unremarkable on any other day—had caught the attention of a nearby officer. Knowing the script, I feigned linguistic helplessness, responding in English to his Russian queries. For a moment, he hesitated. Then, with a wry smile, he said, "My grandmother told me my English lessons would come in handy one day."

We both laughed. I asked how much I owed, paid him on the spot, and drove away.

Not all interactions with officialdom in Russia were as charming, but this one, at least, carried the kind of absurd poetry that made life there unforgettable.

Steven Thunem was chairman of ABN AMRO Russia from 2001 to 2004 and head of VTB Capital Markets from 2006 to 2008.

NIVA QUEEN FOR A DAY
Michele A. Berdy

Every summer from 1992 until I left Moscow in 2022, I followed the age-old Russian tradition of moving out to the dacha. I rented two modest rooms (outhouse at the end of the lot), but it was in an old community just a few kilometers from Rublyovo-Uspenskoye Shosse—Rublyovka—the elite road leading to the residence of the president and other high officials.

Over the years, as the area was built up, two-lane Rublyovka became a traffic nightmare, especially during rush hours. Under Vladimir Putin, the traffic police (*GAI*) seemed to halt cars the moment he shuffled into his morning slippers. The *GAI* would step into intersections, one hand raised, the other gripping a whistle, and freeze thousands of drivers. We sat fuming, checking our watches, tapping on our steering wheels, eyes straining for a sight of the first police cars that heralded the presidential cortège.

During Boris Yeltsin's presidency, the *GAI* only blocked the side roads for about fifteen minutes. One morning in the 1990s, I was driving my Niva (think Jeep, but short and clunky) into the city when I saw the *GAI* preparing to stop traffic. I sped up just enough to slip onto Rublyovka—the last car through before the lockdown.

Ahead of me, the sleek foreign sedans of the new *biznesmeny* sped along the winding road toward Moscow. I stayed close, but when the road widened, they accelerated. Turning onto Kutuzovsky Prospekt, I glanced around.

I was alone.

Not a single car ahead or behind. Just me, rattling along in my maroon Niva—the sole driver on an empty, eight-lane Moscow highway.

You know that dream where you're naked in Times Square? It's nothing compared to this. Tens of thousands of eyes—cops, pedestrians, trapped drivers—watched in silence. I kept an eye on my speedometer—not too fast, not too slow—with quick glances in my rearview mirror. What if the president's cortège came flying up behind me?

I was in a panic until I crossed the Moscow River. Then, suddenly, inexplicably, I relaxed.

This was my moment. For a few glorious kilometers, it was my parade. I nearly waved to the crowds lining the roadside.

Then, just as I turned off Novy Arbat by the Khudozhestvenny movie theater, the presidential cortège roared past.

Perfect timing.

Michele A. Berdy lived almost continuously in Moscow from 1978 until 2022, working in film, translation, communications, and journalism. She wrote The Word's Worth *column for* The Moscow Times *for twenty-two years.*

THE TAXI "CHEK"
Alexander Waechter

I traveled throughout Eastern Europe starting in the mid-1990s and naturally had to grab a taxi at the airport to get to the city center. In those days, grabbing a taxi anywhere was an experience—but nothing like in Moscow. The minute I stepped out of the Sheremetyevo terminal, I knew I was on my own—in a grim, unruly, but exhilarating world.

My first challenge was simply to find a ride. There were no licensed taxis—just "gypsy cabs," ordinary private cars in varying, often deplorable, condition. You'd flag one down, name your destination, and then haggle fiercely over the fare. Fluency in Russian helped. If you didn't speak the language, the price could double—or triple.

In those lean post-Soviet years, many Russians moonlighted as freelance taxi drivers. Occasionally, you'd luck into a corporate car with a chauffeur. Once, I was even driven in what I later learned was a government minister's vehicle.

Fares fluctuated wildly—depending on fuel prices, traffic, the car, or simply the driver's mood. But once terms were set, the journey began in earnest: a hair-raising dash into the city, marked by speeding, ignored lights, pedestrians be damned. All you could do was grip the door handle and hope for the best.

At your destination, you'd be quoted a fare—always outrageous—and promptly ejected. But if you asked for a *chek*—the Russian word for receipt—the atmosphere shifted dramatically.

The driver would stop the car, kill the engine, and solemnly reach for a worn booklet in the glove compartment. Then, with great care, he'd fill out a multi-line form: your departure point, arrival, time, date, his name, his license number. Finally, he would retrieve a small ink pad and stamp the document with an official-looking seal.

The first time this happened, I was stunned. How could the same man who'd just blazed through red lights and charged me three times the going rate now be painstakingly documenting the whole affair? I began to ask for a *chek* every time, just to watch the transformation—from streetwise hustler to miniature bureaucrat.

What explained this odd reverence for paperwork in a city so chaotic? Perhaps it was a relic of Soviet procedure. Or maybe, for a brief moment, even the rogue driver enjoyed playing a role in something official. It's rumored that *cheki* are always issued to certain clients from the security services. But that's another story entirely.

The *chek* may be a local curiosity. But don't we all carry our own ingrained quirks and rituals? It's part of what makes the world so endlessly fascinating.

Alexander Waechter worked in Eastern Europe for CSFB, BNP Paribas, and Citigroup from 1996 to 2012, and lived in Moscow.

SWIFT, UNFORGIVING, AND PAID FOR IN FULL
Douglas Steele

I first came to Moscow in August 1993 with three friends from Halifax, Nova Scotia. After three very eventful days, we decided to open a bar. I made eleven trips before settling in late 1994.

In 1995, I opened my first project—followed by thirty-eight more between 1995 and 2018. I now live in Warsaw with my Russian wife, and we still maintain our home in Moscow.

This is the story of that first project: the Moosehead Canadian Bar. In the 1990s, Moscow was all about connections. Nothing happened unless you knew someone who *knew* someone. To open a bar, you needed a space, partners, and a *roof*—a "security structure" to protect your interests, including from your own Russian partners.

My partners were Jim and John Whelan, two brothers from Newfoundland. On the Russian side was Dmitry Kitchakova, a Kalmyk businessman I'd met through the Dalai Lama's spiritual representative to Russia—a Buddhist monk named Geisha Tingley. Dmitry had ties to the president of Kalmykia and helped us find a property at 54 Bolshaya Polyanka, owned by two Chechen brothers, Achmed and Shariff.

At our initial meeting, we agreed on rent. The investment was to be split 50/50 between our Canadian group and Dmitry. We sourced an American contractor and a Canadian architect. The cost estimate was $350,000.

On the day of the lease signing, Dmitry vanished.

Three days later, we met with the Chechens, who told us they would put up the $175,000 and that we would become partners. But before anything could proceed, our *roof* had to meet their *roof* to "find common ground." The meeting took place. All good. We were partners.

We built the bar, imported all the furniture and fixtures from Canada, hired a Canadian chef from Halifax—and off we went. Seven months later, I left to work on our second project, and Jim Whelan took over day-to-day operations. Within three months, Jim and the Chechens had a major falling out. It got so bad, the Chechens wanted to kill him.

I met with our *roof*, who told me they weren't going to war with the Chechens over Jim. So all parties met and agreed: the Chechens would operate the bar and pay us $20,000 per month.

We never saw a penny.

An expensive learning curve, paid for in full.

Douglas Steele is a Canadian hospitality entrepreneur and advisor with a career spanning more than three decades, including twenty-five years in Moscow, where he led thirty-eight restaurant and nightlife projects, from Hard Rock Café to the iconic Hungry Duck. Since 2018, he has shaped the culinary scene in Warsaw and the Czech Republic with two food halls and ten food-and-beverage concepts.

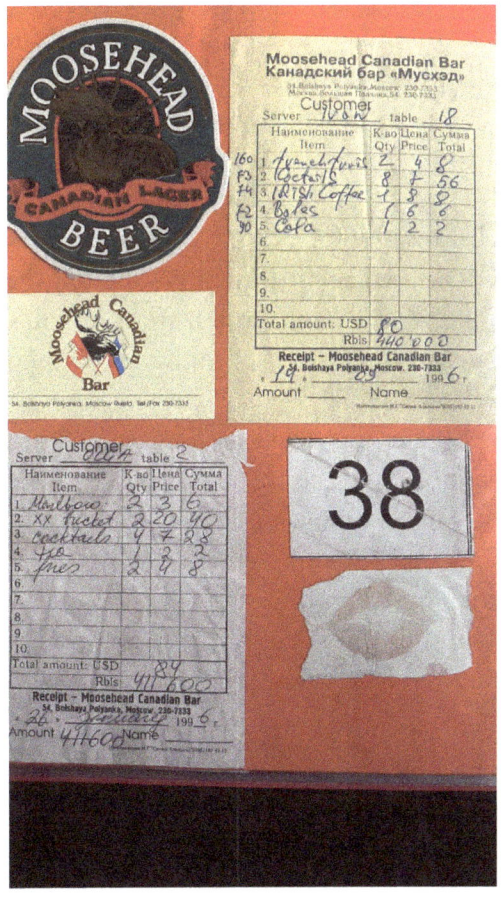

SIBERIAN LEDGER
Richard Creitzman

In the early 1990s, a metals-trading firm sent me across the former Soviet Union—mostly to smelters, coal mines, and chaos. *Our* capitalism was taking its first, confused steps across the Russian landscape.

My work regularly brought me to the Kuzbass coal basin of southern Siberia, which included such delights as Kemerovo, Novokuznetsk, and Novosibirsk. The pollution from the region's metal, coal, and other plants created a smog that enveloped these cities and—apart from the health issues—left the landscape perpetually gray and dull.

Here, the *Sibiraki*—independent, dismissive-of-Moscow-rule *biznesmeny*—were quietly plotting and scheming to thrive in the new economy. One of them, a broad-shouldered, shaven-headed mine owner with no discernible neck, took a liking to me. I was a recent economics graduate from the UK, and he enjoyed our long dinners and vodka-fueled conversations, relishing the novelty of discussing market theories with someone who had studied them formally. One day, he said he wanted to learn more about Western economics, so for my next trip, I brought him a Russian translation of a basic economics textbook, which he was very excited to receive.

About two weeks later, he called me—as usual—to chase an overdue invoice. As we wrapped up the conversation, I asked whether he had taken a look at the book. His reply was immediate, almost triumphant.

"Look?" he said. "I read it all in one day!"

I asked him what he thought.

His response was unforgettable: "Richard, technically—under Western accounting standards—I am bankrupt. But here? *Vsyo normal'no!*" ("Everything is fine!")

It was absurd. And somehow, it made perfect sense.

Richard "Dicky" Creitzman began working in Moscow in 1993, holding senior roles in metals trading, production, and structured commodity trade finance for a leading

German bank before joining one of Russia's largest oil producers as head of corporate finance, where he also participated in the acquisition of a London soccer team. After a brief return to the United Kingdom in 2008, he spent nearly a decade leading finance for three family offices and is now based in Switzerland, reflecting on a thirty-year career.

SILVER STREAK REDEMPTION
Charles Borden

Last we saw Fred, he was outside the Pechatniki City Service for Towed Vehicles in southeast Moscow, having just secured his spot in line by shouting the customary *"Kto posledniy?"* ("Who's last?").

About forty people loitered near the grim building, smoking, complaining, and making occasional runs to the kiosk for a beer, a Snickers, or a sad-looking *shashlik*. Inside, five windows processed paperwork; only two were operational. Fred's car, the noble Silver Streak, sat impounded at a lot far across the city.

Two hours into his vigil, bored of his iPod and crusty snow boots, Fred checked the situation inside. His neighbors had inched forward. Just then: window slam. "Break time." Officially fifteen minutes. Actually, an hour.

By hour four, tensions flared. A line-cutter appeared, triggering a full-blown Moscow-style morality play. One guy took charge like a Soviet hall monitor. Another asked who the hell died and made him queue tsar. Eventually, mob justice prevailed and some vague sense of order returned.

At 20:06—five hours and twenty-six minutes after arriving—Fred approached the window, documents in hand: driver's license with notarized translation, car registration, and a power of attorney form he'd downloaded off some sketchy website. The clerk squinted at it, frowned, shrugged, and finally stamped.

By 20:30, Fred had signed a confession of guilt (refuse, and return in two weeks), and was given a form to pay the 300-ruble fine. The lobby had two ATMs, but both required a Russian driver's license number. Fred did not qualify.

He now had thirty days to pay via Sberbank transfer and mail in the receipt. But first: the car.

The *spets-stoyanka* (special lot) was across the city near the Ochakovo beer factory. Fred hiked to the bus, rode to the Metro, switched lines, rode again, took another bus, and walked down a dark industrial road until, like an apparition, Silver Streak's silhouette emerged.

At 22:15, he rejoined some queue-mates who'd hitched rides. Then the real punchline: the car had been there over 24 hours, accruing a 40-ruble-per-hour fee. Worse: payment had to be made *before* pickup—at Vnukovo Airport.

Fred weighed his dignity. Fifteen minutes later, Silver Streak purred past the gate.

Days later, another expat told Fred he'd just paid a cabbie 3,000 rubles to "handle everything." He got his car in thirty minutes. Fred laughed for a long, long time.

Charles Borden was engaged in Russian agriculture and investment projects and served as editor and writer for dozens of articles and several books for various publications from February 1992 to May 2022.

THE MOST MEMORABLE LOOK & SEE TRIP
Corrado Giaquinto

I've worked as an expat on thirteen assignments, and it was typical to take a look-see trip to arrange housing and get oriented. I expected my look-see trip to Russia to be routine. It turned out to be anything but.

My first encounter with Russia was unforgettable. Our plane landed on an icy November runway with a soprano-worthy screech. Gazing out the window, I saw a bleak landscape of snow and sparse trees—whose leaves had likely fled south months earlier. After clearing immigration, I was greeted by a lineup of elderly men offering taxi services. Despite my repeated refusals, each one gave it a shot, as if I might change my mind because of their charm or persistence.

The drive to the hotel introduced me to Moscow's massive *prospekts*, or boulevards—six lanes wide, though one was blocked by a dead GAZ Chaika abandoned by its owner, another by an accident where drivers waited stoically for the police, and yet another slowed to a crawl by a lumbering truck that might as well have been powered by Fred Flintstone. Roughly three hours later, we arrived at the Sheraton on Tverskaya and rewarded ourselves with our first Russian lunch: blinis and caviar.

Refueled and slightly more optimistic, we set off to hunt for an apartment—just in time for the heaviest snowfall Moscow had seen in 150 years. Getting from the car to the front doors felt like storming Normandy—if Normandy were waist-deep in slush.

Our first encounters with Moscow apartments were, in a word, discouraging. We started to wonder if we'd ever find a decent roof over our heads. The first apartment had a dining room adorned with life-sized Greek statues—strategically posed and, shall we say, anatomically complete. The second featured a golden kitchen installed squarely in the middle of the living room. The third had disco lights built into the ceiling. Between showings, I drifted off in the car, only to wake up and find darkness outside. Had I slept that long? Not at all—it was just 3 p.m.

Despite the rocky start, Russia turned out to be one of my most thrilling assignments, filled with memories I now recall with both affection and laughter. One standout was my first sales convention, where—after downing ten vodka toasts in ten minutes—I was unexpectedly appointed captain of the karaoke team. As the lyrics began to flash on the screen, I realized I couldn't read a single word. I thought I was completely wasted... until it dawned on me that the lyrics were in Cyrillic.

Corrado Giaquinto served as innovation manager for the Central Europe and Russia Division at Colgate-Palmolive in Moscow from 2005 to 2007.

WELCOME TO THE U.S.S.R.: THE SONY STORY
Paul Melling

Mr. Matsuzaki was a man on a mission: to open an accredited office for Sony Consumer Electronics in late 1991. He had three options: the Ministry of Foreign Trade, the Chamber of Commerce and Industry, and the State Committee of Science and Technology. He asked me to arrange meetings with each of them. Sony was a major client, and I was happy to assist.

I had sometimes struggled to build relationships with Japanese clients, but with Mr. Matsuzaki it was different. He had a kind face and a near-permanent smile. But he also bore the responsibility of opening Sony's Moscow office, and nothing was going to divert him.

The first meeting, at the Ministry of Foreign Trade, was overwhelming. It was as if Lenin's grandson had arrived. A small army of fluent Japanese speakers filled the room. Saké was poured. The hospitality bordered on embarrassing. A cascade of "investment opportunities" followed: potential joint ventures, government partnerships, and commercial tie-ins. Mr. Matsuzaki, ever polite, swatted them all aside. He was there for one thing only—accreditation.

The meeting with the Chamber of Commerce followed the same script. The enthusiasm was no less intense, but the tone was softer. It felt like being smothered with a silk babushka shawl while someone gently picked your pocket.

We expected more of the same at our final meeting, with the State Committee.

We were wrong.

The State Committee's office was housed in a forbidding building near Red Square. We arrived on time and were shown to a long, cold corridor, where we waited for more than an hour. No saké. Not even tea.

When we were finally ushered in, two officials listened to Mr. Matsuzaki's presentation in silence, their faces grim. They expressed surprise that Sony would want to open an office in Russia, heaped praise on Sony's competitors, and then summarily dismissed us. Mr. Matsuzaki remained courteous, but I could see he was stunned. I certainly was.

Sony ultimately received its accreditation from the Chamber of Commerce.

A year later, Mr. Matsuzaki explained what had happened. Apparently, some years earlier, Akio Morita—Sony's founder—had visited Moscow and written a book about the experience. In it, he described his visit to the State Committee and remarked that the name was misleading: no one there, he wrote, gave a damn about either science or technology.

The book had been widely read in Moscow.

Our meeting, it turned out, had been payback.

Paul Melling is an English lawyer and the founding partner of Baker McKenzie's Moscow office, where he practiced law from 1989 until its closure in 2022. He served as legal adviser to the British ambassador for most of that period and supported numerous multinational corporations in their business activities in Russia. He is now retired and resides in the United Kingdom.

A MIXED RECEPTION
Richard Dean

I landed in Moscow on February 22, 1988, to open the first American law office in the Soviet Union for Coudert Brothers. Within hours, a line of Soviet citizens eager to air grievances against their own government had formed outside. The authorities shut that down fast—we were there strictly for foreign businesses.

Western media saw our presence as a vote of confidence in Gorbachev's reforms, theoretically welcoming foreign investment. American CEOs certainly seemed convinced and began to fly in en masse. In practice, however, most deals crumbled, and our advice often boiled down to: "Proceed with extreme caution."

With growing visibility came more invitations. As the lone American lawyer in Moscow, I became a sought-after speaker. One memorable request came from a British professor leading a student delegation. I accepted without thinking much about logistics. Since this was a student delegation rather than a high-profile commercial or political group, the professor and his class were placed in a hotel on Moscow's outskirts, far from our downtown office.

I committed to speak, not realizing their hotel was a cartographer's nightmare. Armed with a limited-edition map of Moscow used by U.S. diplomats and purportedly the only accurate map of Moscow available, I set off in the one and only 1987 Lincoln Continental Givenchy in town.

This car was a spectacle. Kids mobbed it at traffic lights, throwing themselves onto the hood in admiration. Progress was slow. To make matters worse, Moscow's outer districts lacked street signs. When I finally stopped to ask for directions, a young Russian took one horrified look at me and bolted—not the response I expected. At the next intersection, I tried a grandmother with two grandkids in tow. Her reaction? "Yes, yes! I will take you there myself!" She and the boys jumped in, and off we went. I suspect she took a scenic detour just to prolong their joyride in this rolling symbol of capitalist excess.

That Lincoln wasn't mine but part of a fleet owned by Swiss firm IPATCO, our sponsor. Back then, foreign law firms couldn't set up shop in the USSR unless an established Soviet business vouched for them. That was impossible for us, so IPATCO's unorthodox arrangement—greenlit at high Soviet levels—got us in.

But back to my odyssey. After an extended tour of Moscow, my impromptu guide delivered me to the hotel. That day, I learned I was either a terrifying enigma or an irresistible attraction—often both. That contrast defined my years in Moscow, but never more vividly than my grand Lincoln adventure.

Richard Dean spent forty-two years as a lawyer with Coudert Brothers and Baker McKenzie. After opening the Coudert office in Moscow in 1988, he was resident there until 1991 before returning to Washington, D.C., to lead the Coudert Russia and Central Asia practice through 2005.

ONE DAY IN AUGUST
Ambassador (Ret.) Eric S. Rubin

In July 2008, I arrived in Moscow to begin my tenure as deputy chief of mission at the U.S. Embassy. Ambassador John Beyrle, my new boss, informed me that he would soon be leaving on vacation. With an encouraging smile, he assured me that he had full confidence in my ability to manage the embassy in his absence. I was grateful for his faith, but an unshakable feeling warned me that there might be surprises in store.

His departure barely made it to the rearview mirror before the first tremors of crisis struck. On August 1, Russian-backed Ossetian militias began shelling Georgian villages—a deliberate provocation. The Georgian government responded with force. Within days, the conflict escalated into a full-scale war.

What followed was a surreal, often painful period. The Russian government orchestrated daily protests, busing in rent-a-crowd demonstrators to chant outside our old embassy building. These staged spectacles persisted for months, a daily reminder that diplomacy in Moscow often was like performance art—only the stakes were dangerously real.

Then, in early November, the theater of the absurd reached its climax. That night, thousands of demonstrators from the pro-Kremlin youth group Nashi gathered outside the embassy, wielding jack-ò-lanterns inked with the names of war victims. As Ellen Barry of *The New York Times* later described it:

> *In a film projected on several large screens, an actor playing President Bush (though with a heavy Russian accent) delivered a speech in which he gloated over the United States' control over world affairs. The film asserted that the United States orchestrated World Wars I and II so that the American economy could overtake Europe's, carried out the Sept. 11 attacks to broaden government powers, and planned to brand every person on the planet with the "mark of the beast," as referred to in the Bible.*
>
> *"When that will happen, we will totally control all humanity," said*

the actor playing Mr. Bush, swigging a beer, as a picture of the globe in chains glowed behind him.

I stood watching, transfixed. It was a nadir in U.S.-Russian relations.

Not long after, President Obama was inaugurated, and the so-called "reset" in U.S.-Russian relations began, leading to a gradual (and short-lived) improvement in ties. But that night, as I watched a Russian actor, perched on a barstool, swigging beer while preaching American world domination, I knew one thing for certain: Moscow had a way of making reality feel stranger than fiction.

Eric Rubin is a retired American diplomat with thirty-eight years of experience. He served as U.S. ambassador to Bulgaria, deputy assistant secretary of state for Europe, deputy chief of mission in Moscow, deputy political counselor in Kyiv, and in numerous other State Department positions.

VLADIVOSTOK: BRIEFINGS, BEATINGS, AND BORDERLINES
Adam A. Blanco

Eight hours and twenty-two minutes after leaving Moscow—crossing seven time zones and more than 6,500 kilometers—we landed in Vladivostok. I was familiar with the journey, having regularly worked with the Vladivostok branch of the Central Bank of Russia. But this visit would be different.

I was joined by two American bankers, Andrew and Doug, who had come to lead a two-day training seminar. The next morning, Viktor, head of the CBR's Primorsky Krai branch, collected us in a convoy of four black Mercedes SUVs, blue lights flashing. Instead of heading to a conference room, we drove straight to the naval port and boarded a sixty-foot yacht. There we met Sergei Darkin—a future governor—who arrived James Bond–style on a speeding water bike and was hoisted aboard by two armed, sinewy bodyguards. The absurdity felt oddly routine.

Later, back at the hotel, we prepared for a two-hour drive the next morning to a remote training center near the Chinese border. Our host, Anatoly—a retired FSB colonel and manager of a Soviet-era *prophylactori* (preventive health center)—greeted us with a firm handshake, a modernized facility, and a schedule more like a luxury wellness retreat than a financial seminar.

That evening, we were invited to the private *banya* reserved for the FSB and Central Bank elite. Coiled sausages, Georgian cheese, and thick black bread were neatly arranged on a table. A muscular *banchik*, armed with birch branches, stood ready to thrash toxins out of us. After the beating, we plunged into a freezing spring and felt, however briefly, immortal.

The vodka flowed like the Volga through the night. Anatoly turned philosophical—then conspiratorial. What began as idle talk about the Chinese border took a darker turn.

"I'll call some friends in Border Patrol," he said. "We'll take a helicopter in the morning to watch hundreds of узкоглазые (uzkoglazye—derogatory, 'narrow-eyed') soldiers—maybe even shoot at a few. A billion Chinese are ready to cross the border."

As the remark was translated, the bankers turned pale.

At breakfast the next morning, Anatoly's sober assistant—mercifully—announced the helicopter trip was canceled. No border, no scandal. Just an oddly choreographed diplomatic stress test. I left with a deeper appreciation for the fine line between ceremony and chaos—and for the quiet *chinovnik* who talks his boss down from a crazy helicopter trip.

It reminded me, too, of enduring Russian anxiety about a billion Chinese reclaiming the sparsely populated Far East—territory ceded to the Tsar by the 1860 Treaty of Beijing, a byproduct of the Opium Wars.

The bankers were disappointed they didn't get their sightseeing tour. But they still talk about that James Bond week in Vladivostok.

Adam A. Blanco lived and worked in Russia from 1992 to 2009 and remains active in the Russian world. He arrived as a Peace Corps volunteer and worked in the Russian private sector across Eurasia.

HALLOWEEN
Eric Luhmann

In 1990s Moscow, expat life demanded imagination—and a taste for the absurd. With the city crackling with opportunity, corruption, and more than a little mystery, even something as simple as planning a Halloween party could take on operatic proportions.

And so it did.

In the summer of 1994, a group of eight expats—restless, ambitious, and perhaps a bit nostalgic for the traditions of home—hatched a plan to stage an unforgettable Halloween weekend. Just not in Moscow. No, we would charter a Russian Yak-42, decorate it like a haunted aircraft, and fly ourselves and eighty fellow adventurers to Bran Castle in Transylvania—better known as Dracula's Castle.

The spectacle began before takeoff. That late October afternoon, Vnukovo International Airport became an unintentional theater. Vampires, skeletons, witches, and werewolves filled the check-in lines, bemusing the Russian staff and fellow travelers. In a cheeky nod to the occasion, our charter flight was listed as Flight 666 from Moscow to Bucharest. The Soviet-style delay—caused by someone awaiting a "facilitation payment"—only gave our monsters more time to begin the party in the sterile glow of the departure lounge.

We boarded the plane already in high spirits, Bloody Marys in hand. The aircraft, oddly enough, was owned by a famed Soviet chess grandmaster, and had been festooned with cobwebs and spiders. During takeoff, some dared to "aisle surf," buoyed by both vodka and bravado, as the plane shuddered skyward.

Moscow, in all its post-Soviet intensity, was always a character in our lives—moody, unpredictable, and deeply vibrant. But stepping outside of it for a weekend, clutching our costumes and flasks, only sharpened our sense of the city's surreal grip. The farther we traveled, the more we saw it clearly: Moscow was not just where we lived—it was the place we had to escape in order to understand.

After that first trip, we made it a tradition, repeating the excursion for three more years. Each came with its own set of complications: military escorts, surprise airport re-routings, even one instance of kissing Romanian passport officers in exchange for expedited entry.

Was it the best Halloween party in Moscow? Technically, no. But for those of us who lived it, there's no contest. It was flight, and freedom and fantastical—all dressed up in vampire capes and fake blood.

Eric Luhmann was a Moscow-based expat from 1994 to 1998 and from 2004 to 2007, serving first as a U.S. diplomat and later as a businessman in the transportation and infrastructure industry.

CHELNOKISM
Joshua B. Tulgan

In 2014, Russia banned the import of a wide range of European Union agricultural products. Polish apples and Irish butter soon disappeared from stores. In many cases, replacements were readily available; Baku tomatoes and Uzbek lemons were far tastier anyway than their Dutch and Spanish counterparts. My wife bought kilos of strawberries to make preserves. When I pointed out that the ban didn't cover her favorite French jam, she shrugged and just ate the berries.

As expected, the surreptitious ban renewed an industry of smuggling—one that should be familiar to any longtime resident of Russia. More formally, a brisk trade in "Belorussian oysters" arose, as Belarus became a conduit for European contraband—in particular, seafood—despite the country's lack of coastline. But informally, we were all effective mules, or, in Russian parlance, *chelnoki*. During my frequent trips to the United States, I was always asked to deliver iPhones and other goods for friends and colleagues that were either hard to find or relatively expensive in Moscow. Necessity, too, compelled action; I once schlepped a duffel bag of diapers back to Moscow for a needy colleague when the ruble crashed in 1998. Later, tight supplies of kosher meat compelled my rabbi to ask that I transport frozen cuts of brisket. When I saw Orthodox Jews gathering in prayer during the flight, I hoped they were offering an orison to ensure my meat-laden suitcases would be delivered before the contents thawed.

The absence of cheese in 2014, though, was a source of much torment. Certain types, like Greek feta, could be swapped for Balkan *brynza*, but the very best cheeses require time. Good cheese is aged—perhaps for years—and is branded as such. The coveted Parmigiano Reggiano is sold in increments of maturity from 24 to 100 months. If an entrepreneurial Russian started making *parmigiano* tomorrow, we realized, it would be years before we saw it legally in Moscow. This is a lifetime to a turophile coping with *caseus* withdrawal. During one trip, I spent over £400 on cheese—so much that they gave me free tote bags to carry it to Moscow.

Before my own wife departed for Moscow last week, she packed a few blocks of English cheddar as gifts for our friends. She transported a stack of documents for others, while a third person asked her to bring some medication. Years later, *chelnokism* remains a thing.

Though born and raised in America, Joshua Tulgan spent over 25 years living and working in Russia, mostly in finance and strategic communications. He and his family live in Dubaisk, UAE.

INVISIBLE BORDERS
Mikki Mahan

In 1989 the Berlin Wall came down and, with it, seemingly, the East–West divide. By the mid-1990s, I had made my way to Moscow after two years with the Peace Corps in Moldova.

From time to time, I traveled back to Moldova to visit friends. It was a two-hour flight from Vnukovo Airport on a Tupolev-154. I had come to expect the distinctive smell of Russian jet fuel in the cabin. I was no longer concerned to see the backs of empty seats flop forward or to hear the passengers break into applause upon landing.

During one of these trips, Vnukovo was undergoing a major renovation. The check-in area had been moved to the middle of a large open space while the work was carried out.

I made my way through the noise and confusion and found the counter for my flight. I handed the agent my ticket, U.S. passport, and Russian visa. She picked up her walkie-talkie and radioed a colleague. "Sveta, I have a foreigner. I need a border."

Apparently, the passport control booths that usually demarcated the border had been temporarily replaced with a roving passport control officer named Sveta. The agent issued my boarding pass but held on to it, along with my documents.

While I waited for Sveta to come and stamp my passport, I tried to look as though I had all the time in the world. I had learned that in the former USSR, any indication you were in a hurry would be rewarded with an even longer wait.

A few minutes later, the agent radioed again: "Sveta, I still need a border." Sveta gave a short response. The agent, exasperated, set down the walkie-talkie.

The line behind me was getting longer. I stepped to the side so she could check in people with Russian or Moldovan passports, for whom a border was not necessary.

After several more minutes, the agent picked up her walkie-talkie again. "Sveta, I said I need a border!"

Sveta's response was unintelligible, but the emotion in her voice came through loud and clear. The agent set down the walkie-talkie, sighed, and looked up at me.

"Do you need a border?" she asked.

"Me?" I paused and then shook my head. "No," I said. "I don't."

She sighed again, handed me my passport and boarding pass, and waved me through the invisible border.

Mikki Mahan lived in Moldova from 1993 to 1996 and in Moscow from 1996 to 2011. She now lives in London.

"WHEN YOUR SON LOOKS LIKE YOUR NEIGHBOR"
Thomas Firestone

I spent eight years at the U.S. Embassy in Moscow, serving under four ambassadors and working alongside figures as varied as Alexei Navalny and Secretary of State Colin Powell. I learned a lot from them, including valuable lessons about how to behave in difficult and politically charged situations. But the piece of wisdom that most echoes in my mind came not from a statesman or political figure, but from a plumber.

After leaving the embassy, I remained in Moscow with a private law firm and had to move from fully serviced diplomatic housing to a private apartment. Shortly after moving in, I noticed that the toilet wasn't working. Not knowing what to do, I reflexively asked one of the embassy handymen for help. He agreed to come by after hours. Out of respect for his time, I offered to pay. He waved it off. I offered again. He waved again.

"You're a good guy," he said with a shrug. "It's OK."

Still, I pressed the point, explaining that it would be awkward—неудобно (*neudobno*)—not to pay him.

He paused, looked at me sagely, and said, "We have a saying in Russian: неудобно is when your son looks like your neighbor. Everything else in life is manageable."

I relented and let him help me free of charge.

I have quoted this aphorism repeatedly not to suggest that we are entitled to commit any kind of social faux pas we please, or to make light of truly serious problems, but to highlight the simple truth that we can often exercise more control over situations than we think—simply by putting them in proper context.

Thomas Firestone is a partner in the Washington, D.C., office of the law firm Squire Patton Boggs. Between 2002 and 2004, and between 2006 and 2012, he served as the Department of Justice resident legal adviser at the U.S. Embassy in Moscow.

GARDEROB
Marc Polonsky

"Besides the English legal system," I would often say, "what we Brits can be most proud of is our theatre."

The English legal system had brought me—with my wife and young family—to Moscow in the summer of 1998. The London-headquartered law firm where I worked was engaged on several large-scale acquisitions and project financings in Russia's hydrocarbon sector, all governed by English law. A Russian speaker, I had been transferred to the Moscow office to work on them.

And now, in late October 1999, the Royal National Theatre was coming on tour, arranged by the British Council. This was an exciting prospect. We all knew of Russians' reverence for Shakespeare and Dickens, and the uplifting power of culture—particularly important in the aftermath of economic "shock therapy" and the August 1998 ruble crash. Knowing nothing about the production (a new play, *Closer*)—the internet was still new, and I hadn't looked up the British press reviews—I bought tickets and invited my office mate and his wife. Dima—a decent, cultured young man with excellent English—accepted enthusiastically.

We trooped into the Mossovet Theatre with the serious anticipation Russians generally feel for cultural outings: men in suits, elderly women leaving their winter coats at the *garderob*.

As it turned out, the play dealt with two couples who swap and cheat, intent on inflicting revenge and pain through sexual jealousy. The embarrassment in the auditorium grew as the plot became clear. The tut-tutting got louder; we could hear the muffled sound of the simultaneous translation emanating from removed earphones. ("The language is as violent and as graphic as you are likely to encounter outside the pages of a porn magazine," *The Times* reviewer had said. "A play full of f- and c-words and juicily explicit descriptions of sex"—*Financial Times*.)

In one scene, people closed their eyes to avoid the text projected onto the screen. (*Financial Times*: "Dan and Larry communicate in near-complete silence on the internet [shown on the backdrop]. Dan, assuming Anna's name and gender, encourages Larry to share dirty (very) sex fantasies and to meet her tomorrow for purposes of anonymous sex; Larry, believing in the dirty talk of this Anna, is very excited.")

After the interval, there were many empty seats, earphones left discarded in bewilderment. So much for the British Council's "shock therapy." To Dima and Masha, I didn't know what to say.

Marc Polonsky first visited the USSR in 1976. He studied in Leningrad in 1981 and lived there again in 1990–91. He later lived in Moscow from 1998 to 2008 and again in 2017–18. His book USSR: From an Original Idea by Karl Marx *(co-written with Russell Taylor) was reissued in 2011.*

MOSCOW NIGHTS
Paul Ostling

We worked like maniacs in a place where the old Soviet rulebook had been tossed, burned, and buried beneath a new and chaotic gospel of hyper-inflation, wild-eyed entrepreneurism, and linguistic bedlam. It was less "Wild West" and more *Mad Max* meets Karl Marx. Dollar signs danced in some eyes, while others still saw the comforting outline of Lenin's Tomb—and no one knew which vision was winning.

Survival required equal parts caffeine, improvisation, and a very flexible definition of "normal." The city was an economy-class rocket ship, duct-taped together and aimed at the moon, fueled by vodka and the desperate dreams of everyone on board.

At night, the pressure valve blew. Some found release at Night Flight—a place so saturated in fantasy it made Vegas look modest by comparison. Aging expats gazed into the bar's endless mirrors, where runway-ready Slavic beauties appeared like a mirage, a miracle no plastic surgeon could match. Somewhere between their third gin and tonic and the fourth rendition of "Simply the Best," these men swore—deep in their souls—they'd morphed into James Bond, Jack Reacher, or, on a bad night, Steven Seagal.

But Night Flight was merely the opening act. True absurdity awaited at clubs like Diaghilev, the crown jewel of Moscow's brief romance with unchecked capitalism. I somehow clawed my way into regular status there—a feat that felt like earning a PhD in ridiculousness. Our table stood grandly at the intersection of the club's T-shaped runway, a vantage point that guaranteed both spectacle and existential crisis.

One night summed it all up: a Spanish rap duo called the Evil Sisters appeared, microphones in hand, ready to deliver … whatever it was they did. The place vibrated with madness. Dancers writhed, drinks flew, and somewhere amid the chaos, a man in a full velvet suit wept—either from joy or the exchange rate.

Diaghilev was a fever dream, the kind of place where you half-expected the chandelier to come crashing down just for dramatic effect. And then—one month later—it did burn down. I watched the smoke rise from my office in the Wave Building, eight floors above Blackberry, and felt a genuine pang of grief. We mourned like we'd lost a beloved, slightly insane relative.

It was 2008. The end of an era. The first domino in a fourteen-year tumble toward the truly absurd.

Paul Ostling was a founding partner of EY's practice in Russia and later served as EY's global chief operating officer. After leaving EY, he led Kungur Oilfield Equipment & Services and Brunswick Rail, and served on the boards of Mobile TeleSystems, PromSvyazbank, Uralkali, Uralchem, MOEX NSD, and Polymetal, among others.

UNRELIABLE MEMORIES
Alistair Stobie

Just over thirty-four years before I wrote this marked the anniversary of the First Gulf War ceasefire. As the old songs have it, we still meet, and stories are told. Truth meets alcohol. Unreliably recounted, here are a few recollections.

It was probably the day after my return from Saratov—when our local *bomzh* (homeless man) watched me pour a bottle of locally produced Saratov vodka into the windshield washer reservoir—that the following events occurred.

Andrei Illych Pannikov was the reason I'd gone to Saratov. He taught me two lessons: never drink the local vodka, and always take a book to a negotiation. Andrei was an interesting character—a KGB officer, persona non grata in Sweden, founder of Lukoil, FTSE 250 director, and—way back—Baring Vostok's first *krysha*, before the cosmonaut and the other KGB guy.

The first lesson is easy: don't go blind early. The second should be universal. We in the West are outcome-driven. From Russia and its provinces to Central Asia, and across much of Africa, I have waited through countless meetings that only began as my departure loomed.

Andrei's instruction was to reverse the narrative. As it turned out, they succumbed; we came out ahead. I took a deal back to Moscow—and a bottle of vodka. The deal, for what it's worth, turned out no better than the vodka.

For the deal to work, the non-negative approval of Mikhail Borisovich Khodorkovsky was needed. Given that this was before 2003, it was still theoretically possible—or at least through Alexei Golyubovich, who, in effect, was one and the same.

Like many long-term Russia hands, when asked for thoughts on Russia today, I have some tired epithets best trotted out with a bottle of wine. But Golyubovich's return to Russia eludes easy explanation—unless you're an old-fashioned cynic and saw a bank account in need of refilling after a gruesome divorce battle.

Eventually, we (Menatep and Baring Vostok) owned tankers together—or at least the equity rights to some tankers and the occasional helping of fresh caviar as the ships made their way north from the Caspian Sea. It took a better man than I to unlock that Gordian knot. But it did make Baring Vostok, from which even better investments came.

Mike Calvey's book sits on a countertop in our kitchen—bookending, as it were, that story.

Timelines are distorted by age itself. All of the above happened—though maybe not in that order.

Alistair Stobie first came to Russia and the former Soviet Union with Baring Vostok Capital Partners. He remained as a partner at Mint Capital and later served as CFO of Volga Gas. He left in 2008 but returned for oil and gas deals, ultimately departing for good after the occupation of Crimea.

STRANGER IN A STRANGE LAND
Peter Enright

In late August 1996, I defected from London to Moscow to work as a cameraman-editor for an independent British TV production company run by a former colleague. My new home: a sixteenth-floor apartment on Akademika Koroleva, the broad boulevard running through Ostankino—Moscow's broadcast hub. It was a serious upgrade from my shoebox flat in London. The windows faced the sky-piercing Ostankino TV Tower, topped by its revolving restaurant and often illuminated at night like a spaceship on a launch pad. The perfect lightning rod for thunderstorm shots.

I was a stranger in a strange land, to borrow a Robert A. Heinlein title. I arrived wide-eyed and illiterate in Cyrillic. Signs reading *PECTOPAH* ("restaurant") appeared everywhere; my friends and I used the word jokingly: "Let's go to the *pectopah*." I learned that *magazin* meant "shop," *piva* meant "beer," and *bardak* meant "clusterfuck"—an apt description of the next five turbulent years.

I shot and edited news and documentary stories across Russia and the former Soviet republics, often under harsh and dangerous conditions—from the Baltics to Kamchatka, through war zones in Chechnya and the frozen Afghan mountains after the 1998 earthquake. Russia tested me at every turn. Surviving meant dodging corruption, enduring bureaucracy, braving the cold, and staying sane. Still, there were compensations: unlikely friendships, late nights at legendary bars, and beautiful, chaotic moments.

I was crash-tackled by a soldier while filming Chechen refugees, survived the Chernobyl radioactive exclusion zone, and froze my ass off in –45 °C weather in Chukotka. I even knelt in bear droppings to get a good angle for a story on orphaned cubs—whose mothers were roused from hibernation and shot by wealthy hunters for "sport."

I filmed inside a mobile nuclear ICBM launcher at a secret base and covered Putin's first election, the Kursk submarine disaster, and countless quiet tales from Karelia to Vladivostok. There were lighter episodes too—being groped by drunk girls at the infamous Hungry Duck and backstage shenanigans with the boy band Na-Na and flamboyant pop icon Boris Moiseev.

Russia isn't for the faint of heart. It's brutal, beautiful, and absurd. It gave me some of the best and worst moments of my life.

I can't return now—it's too risky. As a registered foreign correspondent, I'd likely be labeled a "foreign agent." But one day, when the war ends and speech is free, I'll go back. Moscow, with all its contradictions, remains my favorite city.

Peter Enright is a British-Australian television producer who was based in Moscow for five years, during which time he shot and edited news and documentary stories across Russia and the former Soviet republics. His production work has included reality television shows, music videos, and television commercials.

THE EXCREMENTAL VISION
Dan Goldberg

On March 3, 1992, risking life and limb while hurtling along what was, ironically, deemed a магистраль (*magistral*, "highway") heading from Ryazan to Nizhny, I had my first encounter with Soviet standards of public hygiene outside the capital. The road had been plowed with Soviet efficiency: only the center strip was clear. This forced both our Toyota van and the oncoming semis to balance their right wheels on a narrow ledge of packed ice, six inches above the pavement. Each time we passed another vehicle, mirrors missed by a hair's breadth, the vans tilting inward as if bowing to fate.

Adding to the thrill of the ride was the repeated high-speed dropping of those left wheels into the ubiquitous potholes, causing us to become momentarily weightless—until heads banged against the van roof and shoulder harnesses snapped bodies back to earth. After hours of this, we were thrilled to see a sign announcing площадь отдыха (*ploshchad otdykha*, "rest area"), and ordered the driver to pull in.

Squinting into the low winter sun, we could see a small building, and across the snow I trudged. I had not expected the 1950s-era Whitman Service Plaza on the New Jersey Turnpike, but well before reaching the building my nose was shouting, "Turn back!" It was just a doorless concrete shell with a Third World one-holer in the center.

Worse, the shell was filled to a depth of several inches with torn newspaper and human excrement. I snapped a photo for posterity before making an about-face. With the sun now behind me, I could see that the banks lining the path I had trod were similarly littered with evidence of human necessity—of mixed vintages.

As I reentered the parking lot, a semi pulled in and stopped. The side door opened, and a bulky driver climbed out, grabbed the vertical support bar to the left, deftly spun around, unbuckled and dropped his trousers, extended his backside way out, and relieved himself—thereby saving himself the pointless walk. Discretion prevailed, and I refrained from capturing this final tableau.

And I wondered whether this was truly the superpower that had launched Sputnik, sent Gagarin into space, and terrified the developed world.

Dan Goldberg is a retired senior Russia analyst who served in the U.S. intelligence community for fifty-three years. He is currently an adjunct research staff member with the Institute for Defense Analyses.

SIC TRANSIT GLORIA MUNDI
Steven Solnick

In the summer of 1987, I paid a visit to Dom Knigi, the venerable bookstore on Nevsky Prospect in what was still called Leningrad. I was early in my Sovietological career—just two years into graduate school—and wanted to stock my library with the collected speeches of former Soviet leaders.

I approached a sales clerk and asked in Russian where I might find the collected works of Leonid Brezhnev, who had been general secretary for eighteen years, until 1982. She looked at me oddly.

"Brezhnev?" she asked.

"Brezhnev," I said again, nodding with conviction.

She shook her head slowly, as if I were the village idiot. Then she finally pointed to the shelves around her and said, "We don't have Brezhnev. Now we have G-o-r-b-a-c-h-e-v. Gor-bah-chev!"

Good luck finding any works of Mikhail Gorbachev in a Russian bookstore in the 2020s. "We have Putin now," the clerk would surely admonish you. But there was a moment—captured in this 2008 photograph—when Putin briefly yielded the spotlight, swapping the presidency for the prime ministership with Dmitri Medvedev. Bookstores like this one in Naberezhnye Chelny stored away their Putin portraits and dutifully stacked up the Medvedev ones—just 250 rubles, framed.

The Medvedev interregnum feels, in hindsight, like a bizarre footnote, easily forgotten. But for four years, many of us (inside and outside Russia) debated whether Medvedev could consolidate power and keep Putin sidelined. We collected anecdotes—just as we had eight years earlier about Putin—that the new president was a modernizer, a technocrat. President Obama's team liked working with him and made no secret of it.

Russia, they say, is the land of an unpredictable past. Naberezhnye Chelny was renamed Brezhnev in 1982 to honor him after his death. It recovered its original name in 1988, after Gorbachev went to war against Brezhnev-era stagnation. Three years later, Leningrad was renamed St.

Petersburg, just as the Soviet Union headed for its own demise. In 2011, Kyrgyzstan named a mountain after Vladimir Putin; it stands just a few kilometers from Peak Yeltsin.

Nothing is named for Dmitri Medvedev.

Steven Solnick was an associate professor of political science at Columbia University from 1993 to 2002. He is the author of Stealing the State: Control and Collapse in Soviet Institutions *(Harvard University Press, 1996). From 2002 to 2008, he served as director of the Ford Foundation's Moscow office.*

FORGOTTEN AT THE GATE
Ilkka Salonen

Official Russia today is, at best, wary of foreigners. But that was not always the case. I had the chance—and the pleasure—to see Russia from the inside while working for several banks in the country.

After the 1998 crisis, I returned to Moscow for the third time to lead a bank with majority foreign ownership but a deeply local business profile. Like many others, our bank needed new capital. It wasn't easy, but eventually we persuaded the shareholders that investing in a Russian operation could still be both safe and profitable.

At the same meeting that approved the capital increase, we proposed amendments to the bank's statutes—opening a second front of negotiations with the Central Bank of Russia, a meticulous and demanding regulator. Most of the discussions were handled by our legal teams, until one day our head of legal suggested that I join a meeting with the deputy head of the Moscow branch of the CBR. I agreed without hesitation.

We arrived early on a bitter February morning, the air outside sharp with diesel exhaust and the faint scent of coal smoke. Inside the CBR building, the dimly lit *byuro propuskov*—the pass office—was crowded and cheerless, its walls lined with faded directories and a yellowing portrait of the president.

After a short wait, my colleague received his pass and rejoined me. My wait stretched on. When I stepped up to the window to ask, the clerk—a gray-suited woman with lacquered nails and an expression honed over decades of gatekeeping—told me that no request had been submitted in my name. I politely asked her to check again. Nothing. Eventually, I asked my colleague to proceed to the meeting and explain the situation.

He returned soon after, slightly amused. "Our host was embarrassed," he said. "They had forgotten that Ilkka is a foreigner and hadn't submitted his name for security clearance."

I was, of course, frustrated—but also, oddly flattered. Absurd as it may seem today, there had been a time when I could blend in. In that moment, I felt I belonged in a way that went beyond paperwork.

Soon enough, my name was called and the pass was issued. The meeting itself was cordial and productive. I couldn't help but feel that our host's momentary embarrassment had nudged the outcome in our favor.

The days when Russia was opening to foreigners are now gone. One can only hope those days return—when being a foreigner in Russia felt less foreign.

Ilkka Salonen spent approximately twenty years working in Russia's financial sector, holding senior positions at International Moscow Bank, Sberbank, and Uralsib. He served as CEO of both International Moscow Bank and Uralsib, and as deputy CEO of Sberbank.

V

HUMILITY

What are you laughing at? You are laughing at yourselves!

Чему смеётесь? — Над собой смеётесь!

Nikolai Gogol, The Government Inspector
Николай Гоголь, Ревизор
1836

RUSSIA FOR ME
Jonathan C. Knaus

The L-shaped kitchen table is covered with plates of pickled garlic cloves and shoots, potato salad, sliced beef tongue, and *shuba*—herring under a fur coat, layered with beets. My wife, Viktoriya, and I sit at one end with our backs to the wallpaper. Andrei Mikhailovich is tending to two Russian wolfhounds that stood nearly waist-high but looked narrow as a beam. Larisa is preparing to take the baked fish out of the oven. Their children—Seriozha, Pasha, and Katya—move in and out, tasting food, though mostly it's the four adults at the table, toasting vodka and talking about life.

We sit for hours—joking, laughing, and exchanging thoughts about the world. Four minds searching for a common language; four souls sharing joy and heartache.

I first met Andrei Mikhailovich and Larisa at the open-air market in Izmailovo in 1991. Andrei was selling small lacquer boxes he had painted himself. He also painted beautiful *matryoshka* dolls and eggs adorned with scenes from famous icons. We became friends immediately and would meet once or twice a year—a friendship that lasted more than twenty years during my time in Russia.

Andrei and Larisa once took our family mushroom hunting. You can only imagine a foreigner traipsing through the middle of a dense Russian forest, trying to tell the difference between edible mushrooms and *paganki* (the poisonous kind). At one point, after responding to a silly call—"Woohoo!"—I stumbled off in a vodka-fueled haze, trying to find the campfire where everyone had gathered. I was certain I was lurching deeper into the woods, destined never to be found.

My memories of Russia are filled with evenings spent in warm kitchens, drinking vodka and *Tarkhun* (tarragon soda), and chewing on pelmeni, herring, and pickled cucumbers. At first, my Russian was so poor I could barely follow the conversation. But after twenty years of study and practice, I was able to take part in truly wonderful and intense discussions.

I enjoyed the embassy balls, the American Chamber dinners, and the many expat gatherings. But Russia, for me, will always be the long afternoons and nights—raising toasts, sharing belly-shaking laughter, and listening to Russian dance music with close friends. Some of those dear friends are gone now, but I'll always cherish the memories we made together.

Jonathan Knaus worked in Moscow from April 1991 to August 2011. He held positions with Aeromar Joint Venture (Marriott Corporation and Aeroflot), Unisys, Eastman Kodak, American Express, and Western Union. His late wife, Viktoriya, was Russian, and he has two children, both born in Moscow.

THE BANYA DRIVES ANY AILMENT FROM THE BODY

Ambassador (Ret.) Allan Mustard

Watching TV one lazy Saturday in Moscow, I stumbled upon a children's cartoon series about Russian history. The episode dealt with False Dmitry, the Polish pretender to the Russian throne who contributed to the Time of Troubles. One of the cartoon's chief indictments of this treasonous pseudoruler was that "he didn't like the Russian *banya*."

Obviously, anyone who doesn't like the *banya* can be neither Russian nor a Russophile. The *banya*'s role in society extends far beyond the traditional New Year's Eve screening of Eldar Ryazanov's classic film *The Irony of Fate, or Enjoy Your Bath!*—or even the need for a good scrubbing. The *banya* is to Russian businessmen what the golf course is to Western entrepreneurs: the place for serious conversations that lead to the mutual trust underpinning handshake deals.

Since steaming in the *banya* involves stripping naked, it also assures both sides that no one is wearing a wire. For gatherings of old friends, a high-end *banya* is the combination billiard hall, watering hole, massage parlor, and social club where one can let her or his hair down—literally—while effortlessly letting the hot, moist air relax the muscles.

My first encounter with the *banya* came while studying in Leningrad, where the university dormitory turned on the hot water only while students were in class. We sissy Americans took to the *banya* for our hot baths and showers. In later years it became a fixture of my sojourns in Russia, for both socializing and hygiene. On a field trip to Primorsko-Akhtarsk, my host offered a choice: a lush banquet in the town's best restaurant, or an evening in a shoreline *banya* that had the Azov Sea as its swimming pool, with crawdads and beer on the menu.

You can guess which I picked.

Allan Mustard first visited the USSR as a student in 1978 and later served as an American diplomat in the USSR, the Russian Federation, and Turkmenistan.

THE BLUE LIGHT OF RUSSIAN SOULS
Marie de La Ville Baugé

When the wind sweeps across Russia's frozen roads, it lifts veils of organza that flee at the approach of a vehicle. As the polar night retreats and daylight filters through, the white expanse transforms into an endless palette of blues—navy, petrol, steel gray, icy silver—sometimes pierced by that oblique northern light. From my travels, I have carried this light with me, a blue light that, to me, holds the essence of the Russian soul.

For beyond the landscapes, Russia has offered me a deeper lesson: solidarity in adversity. I have seen it raw and unyielding, from war-scarred Chechnya to the most remote tracks of my expeditions.

In the depths of the Arctic darkness, I drove the roads of the Kola Peninsula. In Kolyma, in the heart of winter, I traveled the two thousand kilometers of the "Road of Bones," built at the cost of thousands of prisoners' lives. For days at a time, one might see only a single vehicle. Out there, the rule is simple: when the temperature drops below –40°C, if a car is stopped, you stop. You help.

A truck driver once told me how he saved a man stranded at –55°C—twelve hours spent repairing the vehicle together in a cold that shows no mercy. In the Kola Peninsula, my friend Dima, a police officer, rescued two men whose car had broken down. They had set out without coats, trusting in their vehicle's heating. Only after bringing them to safety did he realize they were criminals. But in Russia, even between a policeman and a thief, saving a life comes before all else.

I have met such guardian angels even on the frozen immensity of Lake Baikal. The day our UAZ sank through the ice in the heart of that white desert, our guide acted within thirty seconds—pulling us out of the vehicle, improvising slippers from a sleeping bag, wrapping us in his jacket. Saving us.

Russia, to me, is also this: a rebirth, somewhere within the blue waters. Since then, I have never ceased to paint this blue light of the soul.

Marie de La Ville Baugé is a nomadic visual artist. Originally from France, where she grew up surrounded by artists, she worked in Cambodia, Sudan, Russia, and is now in Portugal.

ENDLESS SHADES OF GREEN
Sarah Waybright Barr

In August 1999, we trekked into the Siberian taiga west of Baikal, the world's deepest lake and the keeper of one-fifth of Earth's fresh water. Our group was an unlikely mix: Russian teens and elders, three American environmental science graduates, a German PhD student, and two Siberian hunters—wielding rifles to protect us from bears. As the sole American who spoke Russian, I was there with the Tahoe Baikal Institute to guide a ten-day ecological backpacking trip for local teens.

As we packed in the school gymnasium, the elders handed us suspicious cans of meat to carry.

"And where do we put the cans when they're empty?" I asked.

One reached for a frayed Soviet "how-to" manual and pointed to the section on burying waste in the woods.

A Soviet military vehicle with tires taller than I was dropped us deep into the forest. There was no trail. We moved in a single-file line over thick moss in the direction of the Kitoi River—or so I was told. It felt like we were walking in circles.

Early one morning midway through our hike, I stumbled out of my tent and found myself surrounded by endless green—firs and ferns contrasted against the gray stillness. One of the hunters, Anatoly Ivanovich, stirred mushrooms and dill into breakfast soup. His face was weathered and warm under a wool cap. He poked at my perpetually damp boots, steaming near the fire.

"I know you're frustrated," he said in Russian. He'd witnessed my debates with the elders.

"Our families were sent here by Stalin. We adapted. This land will outlast us both. You're here to share what you know—how to be better stewards of the land. But in the end, we're small. *Pozhivyom–uvidim*. Let's live—let's see."

He was right. And the truth was, I couldn't survive without them. There were no maps, but the hunters knew every fold of the hills. As we foraged for mushrooms and berries to supplement our food, the elders taught us what was safe to eat.

Around our campfires, I found Anatoly Ivanovich was not only a storyteller but also an artist, who had studied fine art years ago. He sketched in my journal so I would remember our trek deep within the taiga. And each night, as the stillness enveloped our eclectic group, we sang "Kalinka," our voices carrying into the infinite green.

Sarah Waybright Barr first visited the Soviet Union as a Peace Child in 1991. She studied abroad in Yaroslavl and was a fellow with the Tahoe Baikal Institute upon graduating from Middlebury College. Eager to live and work in Russia, she moved to Moscow in 2000 and began her design career by leading the rebrand program of Aeroflot Russian Airlines. She is currently working on a memoir about finding hope and home in the most unlikely of places—Russia.

Original drawing by Anatoly Ivanovich. August 1999

FOREIGNERS, FAR AND NEAR
Catherine Breen

"Penguins!" shouted the student excitedly, as she peered out the frost-covered window of our weathered UAZ van. A star pupil in her second year of law school at the local state university, Sveta had joined our team as an intern on a U.S.-funded agricultural land privatization project. We were headed to a collective farm where we would conduct our next privatization auction, allowing locals to acquire ownership of land plots and equipment through a voucher system.

As we rumbled alongside the frozen Volga River, another student leaned over and said, "Those are not penguins, silly girl. Those are men hunched over ice fishing." All the students in the van laughed. Sveta stuck out her lower lip and sat back in her seat. With her high-heeled boots, long red nails, and ruffled silk blouse, she seemed more out of place in this van than I—a young American from the suburbs of Boston, whose main experience with agriculture had been selling fresh produce at a summer farm stand as a teen. I spoke fluent Russian, however, and was dressed appropriately for the subzero temperatures. Bundled in my mom's battered fur coat from the 1970s, rabbit *ushanka* pulled down tight over my ears, and heavy snow boots, I painted a near-perfect picture of a young Soviet bureaucrat. So much so that when we arrived at the farm, the locals mistook me for one of their own and pulled me aside.

"How could you let this young American dressed like a hooker come to tell us what to do with our land?" the farmers asked. "Do you really think she can help us?" they snorted. "Is she married?" another from the crowd shouted. "I would like to move to America!" Everyone laughed. I explained that the student interns, including Sveta, were from the local university and were, in fact, there to help the farmers.

As the day unfolded, the students huddled with the farmers in the drafty meeting hall, furrowed brows betraying the effort of translating the thick privatization manuals into practical advice. The farmers, skeptical at first, bombarded them with questions—some pointed, some laced with good-natured teasing. But as Sveta expertly explained how the vouchers could be combined to buy larger plots, her long red nails tapping the table for emphasis, the mood shifted. "These Americans," one farmer finally admitted, rubbing his stubbled chin, "they're not just here to steal from us."

Catherine Breen worked in Moscow and Nizhny Novgorod for the International Finance Corporation (IFC) from 1993 to 1998. She returned to Russia several times thereafter, most recently in the fall of 2017.

THE BETTER PART OF VALOR
Matthew Roazen

My wife and I came to Russia when our two oldest children were in day care. By the time they were ready for legally mandated formal instruction, I did not yet have a pay package that would cover the embassy school. Rather than shell out tens of thousands of dollars per child per year so they could play with blocks and crayons in English, we donated 1,000 rubles a month in cash to Detsky Sad No. 1917, and the boys were enrolled in the beginning stages of what would become a decade of Russian-language education. We told No. 1917's *zavuch*—the principal—to separate the two of them into each of the tiny school's two sections so they couldn't hide in a corner and speak English to one another.

For three weeks, our little redheaded, apple-pie brats came home crying in frustration at their linguistic isolation from the other children—until one day they came home smiling and told me, in perfect Russian, that (a) the class had a new pet turtle named Pashka, and (b) I could go eat a bowl of horseradish.

By the time they were ready for first grade, the boys could read and write in the target language at the same level as their native peers. Once they graduated from kindergarten, I enrolled them—for a slightly higher monthly donation—at School No. 1239, an elite English-language Russian public school. The only class actually taught in English was English—and a very English English at that.

I once went to complain to No. 1239's *zavuch* that my little Yanks had been marked down from a 5 to a 4 in their native language simply because they refused to say *aluminium* or write *colour*. The woman simply shrugged and pointed to the huge photograph behind me. I turned to see a picture of Queen Elizabeth II herself, standing in the school's courtyard sometime in the previous decade, grinning from ear to ear as tiny first-grade girls with huge white bows in their hair offered Her Majesty a massive bouquet of white, blue, and red roses.

Caught between two queens, I simply shrugged like a wise knight in surrender and told the family, "When in Third Rome . . ."

Matthew Roazen may have been the first American lawyer to work for the U.S. offices of a Russian law firm. From 1997 to 2013, he lived in Moscow with his wife and their two—later four—children, where he practiced law for various companies and firms. For the past ten years, he has been in private practice in the United States.

THE MOVERS
Stuart Lawson

In November 1995, fresh from Milan, we were settling into our new Moscow apartment—a sprawling, 400-square-meter residence that had once belonged to Vyacheslav Molotov, Stalin's infamous foreign minister. Situated just a stone's throw from the Kremlin, it was a stark reminder that communism had been anything but egalitarian. The apartment's luxurious wood paneling, Molotov's original paintings, and books spoke volumes about the privileges of the Soviet elite.

Had I known more about Molotov—his ruthless loyalty to Stalin, even sending his own wife to the camps—I might have thought twice about living there. But we were swept up in the thrill of our Russian adventure, eager to embrace the history and opportunity of this chaotic "Wild East" market.

Winter had arrived, snow blanketing the streets as the movers pulled up in their van. Inside were the belongings of our lives—worldly possessions that had journeyed across continents. The movers, a cheerful crew, wasted no time hauling boxes into the apartment.

I've always found unpacking to be an oddly delightful ritual—like an unseasonal Christmas, rediscovering forgotten treasures. Though not always pleasant—a farewell party in Cairo once resulted in cling-film-wrapped ashtrays and half-empty glasses arriving in Paris, exuding the stench of regret.

After hours of work, the foreman asked for a break. Happy to oblige, I offered to make coffee. When I returned, steaming mugs in hand, I froze at the scene before me: two movers perched on crates, a third between them, all engrossed in a game of chess. Mozart played softly on my boombox.

I marveled at this display. "What a country," I thought, "so cultured that even movers play chess to classical music." The anecdote became a staple at dinner parties, earning smiles and nods of admiration from foreign friends.

Years later, recounting the tale to a Russian acquaintance, I noticed his bemused expression. He let me finish, then said, with a mix of incredulity and pity, "You thought they were just movers? They were probably doctors, scientists, or teachers. By the mid-'90s, people like them couldn't find work anywhere else."

The realization hit me like a punch to the gut—a humbling reminder of Russia's turbulent transition, where brilliant minds were reduced to survival jobs, their dignity intact, their talents waiting for a better day. How little I had understood of the quiet sacrifices and resilience that defined the Russia we had entered—a land where intellect and culture battled daily against uncertainty and loss.

Stuart Lawson was CEO of Citibank Russia in 1995 and spent twenty-five years in senior roles across the banking sector, including at Delta Bank, Menatep, Soyuz, and HSBC. He later served for eleven years as a senior adviser at EY and was a director of Skolkovo Ventures, the British Chamber of Commerce, and the Association of European Businesses. He lectured widely on leadership and was a professor at Plekhanov University. He left Moscow in January 2022.

VI

DESOLATION

Russia will be silent, mute and cold, like the grave.

Россия будет молчать, безмолвная и холодная, как могила.

Fyodor Dostoyevsky, Demons
Фёдор Достоевский, Бесы
1872

FOUR HUNDRED COWS, NO FISH
Anders Åslund

From 1984 to 1987, I served as a Swedish diplomat in Moscow, reporting on the Soviet economy to the Swedish Ministry for Foreign Affairs. The Soviet authorities made it clear that Western diplomats were expected to remain in Moscow and limit their activities to meetings at the Ministry of Foreign Affairs (MID). But I was determined to travel and see more of the country for myself.

We were allowed to move freely only in Moscow itself. Most of the Soviet Union was closed to foreigners, but we could request permission to visit certain places, which I did frequently. Each trip required meticulous planning—flights, hotels, and a detailed program. About every second time, however, a man would call forty-eight hours in advance and state, *Vasha poyezdka ne razreshayetsya!* ("Your trip will not be allowed!") before hanging up without saying who he was or why my trip was prohibited.

Official delegations were a safer bet; these visits were rarely denied and often provided valuable insight. In November 1986, I served as interpreter during the annual Soviet–Swedish fishing negotiations in Tallinn. As part of the program, we toured what was described as the finest Soviet fishing kolkhoz. Back in Moscow, I had already learned that fresh fish had largely disappeared from shops since the mid-1960s. Stores were filled instead with barely edible canned fish. Why? My Estonian hosts explained that selling fresh fish wasn't profitable for them. The more heavily processed the product, the higher the official state price—and the greater the revenue for the kolkhoz. So they focused on canned goods, regardless of quality or public preference.

On another occasion, I visited a large agricultural sovkhoz in the Moscow region. My hosts proudly reported a major increase in labor productivity following the construction of a new cowshed: six milkmaids could now milk four hundred cows. However, total milk output had fallen by a third. The reason? The cows spent so long waiting in line to be milked that they had far less time to graze.

In everyday Moscow shops, only a few items could reliably be found in acceptable quality: rye bread, mineral water, salt, and vodka. That was the extent of dependable consumer goods in a supposed global superpower. It is no surprise that the Soviet Union eventually collapsed. The real miracle is that it managed to persist for as long as it did.

Dr. Anders Åslund served as a Swedish diplomat in Moscow from 1984 to 1987 and was an adviser to the Russian reform government from 1991 to 1994. In 1989 he published Gorbachev's Struggle for Economic Reform *(Cornell University Press).*

SIBERIAN OIL
Kevin McKinney

White Nights claimed the distinction of being the first U.S.–Soviet business joint venture. With headquarters in Houston, its mission was oil production in Tyumen, northwestern Siberia, where it operated offices in Raduzhny, Nizhnevartovsk, and Novoagansk. I was part of the logistics team, responsible for managing the importation of all rig office equipment—a role that inevitably involved building relationships with local authorities.

After spending considerable time at the rail yard in Nizhnevartovsk, I had become well acquainted with the head of customs, Gennady, the *man*. One day, several containers of office furniture and copy machines arrived, prompting an urgent summons. "This isn't a telephone conversation," Gennady said. When I arrived, he was waiting with his friend—the head of the regional tax inspectorate.

They had done their calculations. The official duty on the contents of our shipment came to $1.8 million. But they had a proposal. In exchange for a copy machine valued at just over $100,000, Gennady's friend would erase the bill entirely.

I felt my stomach tighten. This wasn't some backroom whisper or subtle hint—this was a direct proposition, spoken without hesitation, as though it were the most natural thing in the world. I kept my face neutral, my mind scrambling for the right response. I told them I would relay the offer.

Sensitive business is never conducted electronically, so I drove to headquarters in Raduzhny to present the offer. The response was swift and unequivocal: "No! We don't bribe." Some paper-pusher dutifully recited the Foreign Corrupt Practices Act, his voice deliberate, as if reading from a script. I assumed the room was bugged, so I jotted the request on a slip of paper and took it directly to the general manager. He crumpled my note without a glance and handed me a printed copy of the FCPA.

They had come to Russia expecting to operate without bribes?

I drove back to Nizhnevartovsk, preparing for the fallout.

Gennady was equally incredulous when I relayed the rejection. He assumed I had failed to explain the offer properly. "You don't understand," he said. "My friend is the highest-ranking official here. There is no possibility of criminal recourse." Then, shaking his head, he asked, "What's wrong with Americans?"

White Nights went bankrupt. The parent company later attributed its collapse to the Russian government imposing tariffs far beyond what had been agreed. Economists, lawyers, and accountants have since demonstrated that strict adherence to the Russian tax code can result in obligations exceeding 140 percent of a company's income. As the old Russian saying goes, *The severity of our laws is mitigated by lax enforcement.* But for those who insist on obeying them—watch out!

Kevin McKinney studied Russian language, history, and culture at George Washington University and Leningrad State University. Based in Moscow for nearly twenty years, he has traveled to nearly every region of the former Soviet Union. He began casually writing what would become Sovok *in March 2021 as a compilation of his experiences. The war in Ukraine prompted him to publish the book, offering insights into why the world's second-largest military has proved so profoundly incompetent.*

THE RISK OF SUCCESS
Matthew Murray

After three months, my Russian partners and I had nearly completed delivery of over 3,000 tons of American food aid to hospitals, orphanages, and schools in St. Petersburg. It was 1992, and Russia was in a humanitarian crisis due to the collapse of its food distribution infrastructure. The former Soviet state-controlled system was in disarray and had yet to be replaced by a functioning private sector. Vulnerable populations were not receiving adequate nutrition. The Russian government had requested U.S. assistance to fill the gap.

We met to conduct a final inventory of deliveries. Out of thousands of boxes—each packed with rice, beans, and flour—only one was missing. The Russian manager smiled and led me outside to his Zhiguli. In the trunk was the missing box, which he said he'd deliver to a nearby school that day.

I had arrived in St. Petersburg in October 1991 and formed a joint venture called the Bronze Lion. Our registration was signed by Vladimir Putin, who was then serving as head of the Committee for External Relations in the office of Anatoly Sobchak, the mayor.

Bronze Lion's first major undertaking was managing this humanitarian aid contract with the U.S. Department of Agriculture. We were responsible for offloading, storing, and distributing the food, working with the St. Petersburg Administration to reach those in greatest need.

In designing the operation, I looked to Herbert Hoover's example as head of the American Relief Administration during the Russian famine of 1921–22. To guard against diversion and black-market sales, he pioneered a direct "port-to-mouth" system. I adapted this model to 1992 Russia with help from my Russian partners—former Soviet engineers who had built a disciplined community around a karate school.

When the final shipment was complete, we met with the St. Petersburg Administration to report. Vladimir Putin sat at the head of the table, questioning why the U.S. was providing food aid. Our explanation—that the

Russian government had requested help and America had responded with generosity—left him unmoved.

Putin then asked if more food aid was coming. Enthusiastic, we told him that USDA had asked Bronze Lion to manage more shipments. In response, Putin declared that he would now personally oversee all future distribution of American aid.

The room went silent. I had a sinking feeling that our success had turned Bronze Lion from a model partner into a perceived threat—and even a potential target.

Matthew Murray first visited the Soviet Union in 1987 as part of an American bicycle tour. He lived and worked in Russia from 1991 to 2002 and again from 2007 to 2009 as a lawyer, entrepreneur, business executive, and cofounder of an NGO.

KOMI STORY
Jan Dauman

Between 1991 and 2011, I visited some twenty-five Russian towns and cities. Despite their unique histories and cultures, one trait was universal among locals: a survival mentality shaped by seventy years of Soviet rule. Trust extended only to a tight circle of family and friends, with loyalty to this group taking precedence over all else.

This mindset was crucial to understanding business in post-Soviet Russia, where the economy teetered on chaos and broken supply chains turned even the simplest transactions into exercises in endurance. Nowhere was this clearer than in the pharmaceutical industry. The once-centralized distribution system had collapsed, and getting medicine to those who needed it became a logistical nightmare.

A consortium of three international pharmaceutical companies enlisted me to help build a best-practice distribution company—starting with a single region before expanding nationwide. We chose Komi, an autonomous republic 1,000 kilometers north of Moscow, largely due to existing relationships.

Komi had long been synonymous with exile. During Stalin's era, its frozen tundra was a graveyard for prisoners, and many of their descendants still lived there. When I asked locals why they didn't leave, the answer was always the same: "To where?" Moscow was unaffordable, and in Vorkuta, at least, they had jobs, food, heat, and a community—though most of their children had moved away.

Komi's president, Yuri Spiridonov, styled himself *malen'kiy* ("little") president out of deference to Boris Yeltsin. A lifelong Communist in his late fifties, he struggled with the new economic realities but was determined to revive Komi's fortunes. He was enthusiastic about our project, offering unwavering support as we designed modern logistics, operations, and governance structures suited to the region's harsh conditions.

Months of preparation led to a final meeting for Spiridonov's signature. Everything was in place—facilities designed, investments secured, permits granted, staff trained. Then, never previously mentioned, he introduced one last requirement: a covert pricing mechanism had to be implemented to divert ten percent of each contract to the health minister—his close friend. The commitment, he assured us, had already been made.

He was puzzled by our resistance. To him, this was business as usual. When we explained it was illegal, he seemed genuinely surprised. Despite weeks of ensuing discussion, he insisted his loyalty left him no choice.

Ultimately, the consortium withdrew, and the project unraveled. It was a sobering lesson in Russian business culture: personal loyalty could outweigh not just economic progress but even the best-laid plans for change.

Dr. Jan Dauman is the founder and CEO of InterMatrix Group, with affiliates in twenty-five countries. He has more than forty years of experience working with leading multinationals on international strategy, business development, and M&A. In 1991, he founded InterMatrix Russia. He has made more than two hundred business trips there until 2013, supporting multinational clients and local entrepreneurs.

THE RULES UNWRITTEN
Topper Power

I arrived in Moscow in the summer of 1995 with the MBA Enterprise Corps—fresh out of business school and eager to take part in Russia's post-Soviet transformation. After a month of language training, I was sent to Vladivostok with Deloitte & Touche under a U.S. Agency for International Development (USAID) initiative to support local entrepreneurs. It was an intoxicating time—optimism and uncertainty in equal measure. A year later, I returned to Moscow to work for Andrei Nechaev, former economy minister under Yegor Gaidar, who had taken control of a small state-owned bank.

My role at the bank was loosely defined—part financial prospecting, part troubleshooting unexpected business ventures. I worked on real estate investments and tried to sell the bank's stake in Severstal, a Soviet-era steel mill. Foreign investors hesitated, wary of legal ambiguities, decaying infrastructure, and the sheer improbability of the pitch. We were ahead of our time, chasing deals in a country still grasping at capitalism's meaning.

Nechaev—more professor than banker—arrived at the office toward evening, summoning me past midnight for discussions on macroeconomics. He paced his wood-paneled office, rolling two glass marbles in his palm, a cigar smoldering between thoughts. My circle expanded. Oleg, a charismatic retail banker, became a close friend; our nights were spent exploring Moscow's bars and debating politics. Mark, a British trader importing Quaker Foods products, introduced me to the city's eclectic cultural undercurrents.

One day, Nechaev introduced me to Norman, an American investor locked out of his own company, Finval. His Russian partners had seized control while he was abroad. When he returned, armed guards blocked his entry. Calls went unanswered. He had been erased. Norman wanted a solution—one that avoided violence.

Oleg introduced us to Bastion, a private security firm led by Elena Andreeva—a rarity, a woman running a security outfit in Russia. Unlike criminal "protection" rackets, Bastion was disciplined and professional. Elena proposed a forceful yet legal operation to reclaim Finval. Norman hesitated. His American investors, horrified by the prospect of physical confrontation, declined. They chose to walk away. Norman soon left Moscow and never returned.

It was a lesson in power—not just in Russia, but in business itself. Western investors believed contracts would protect them. Russian partners knew better. In a system without reliable institutions, control belonged to those who held the keys. Moscow in the 1990s was a place of vast possibilities and profound risk. It was not about right or wrong but about adaptation—learning the rules as they were, not as one wished them to be. And in that, perhaps, there was something universal—a truth that extended far beyond the Russian capital.

Post-Soviet Moscow taught Topper Power to navigate high-risk, unpredictable environments—skills that later enabled him to arrange numerous telecom infrastructure financings across Russia for Lucent Technologies and to build a successful career applying financial and political risk expertise in other emerging markets.

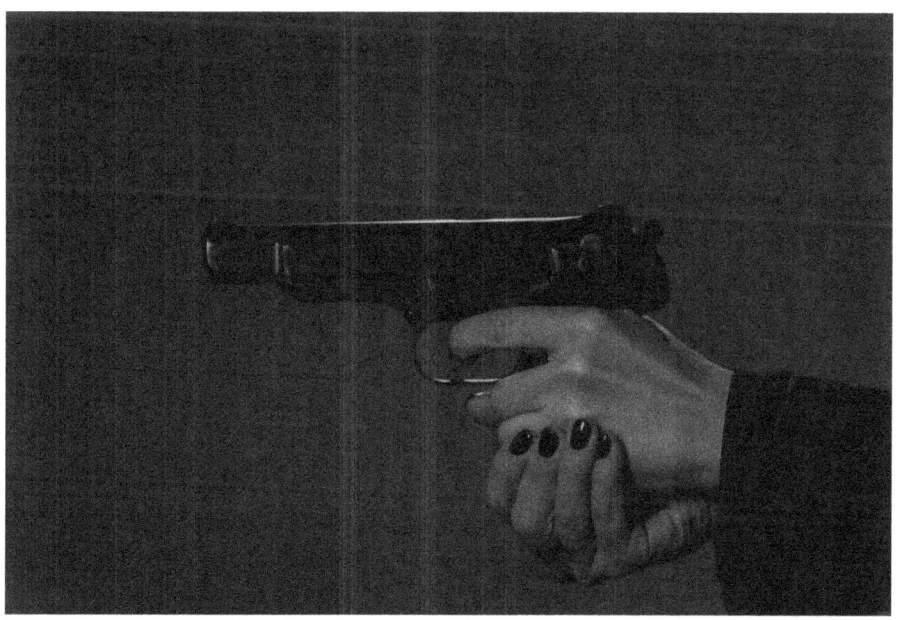

OF COLD VODKA AND HOT BANYAS
Steven Parker

The steam in the Sochi *banya* blurred everything, as did the copious glasses of ice-cold vodka. Somehow, in a single evening—after the private jet flight from Moscow, sweating in an exclusive Russian steam house wearing nothing but traditional felt caps; after eating caviar on blini—we had struck a deal that would shape sponsorship of the Sochi 2014 Winter Olympics. It was 2:30 a.m., and we all stumbled to bed.

The next morning my body still glowed from the birch-branch thrashing and the sting of alcohol. At breakfast, no one could remember what we had negotiated—except, it seemed, me. I could have fabricated our discussion, but instead I reeled off the seven or eight key principles we had agreed to the previous night: to be partners in the upcoming Sochi 2014 Winter Olympic Games.

It had all started six months earlier, when X-Bank realized they had misspent a great deal of money and that what they thought they had paid for in local sponsorship rights was not theirs to command—and that many of those rights belonged to us, as worldwide sponsors. Their initial reaction was: "If you don't play with us, you'll never operate in this market again!" Their final moves were a very Russian charm offensive—with *banya* and vodka—in order to negotiate a bilateral agreement in ways never attempted before—or since—for an Olympic commercial partnership. We signed the deal formally on a snowy slope in Vancouver, a few weeks after the flight to Sochi.

In the couple of years that ensued, we were invited to Olympic parties with then prime minister Putin as master of ceremonies in the old Kremlin stables. We attended a concert in Sochi with President Medvedev and his favorite Russian rock band, B2. We were guests at glittering receptions in palaces and museums across St. Petersburg. Of course, the Sochi Olympics culminated in the invasion of Crimea, sanctions, and the ejection of all international players from the local payments system—despite more than twenty years of local operations by U.S. companies in Russia.

It remains difficult to explain what it's like to do business in Russia—and, more importantly, how deals and partnerships are actually built. To help our American chairman understand, we introduced him to a seasoned U.S. entrepreneur in St. Petersburg. When asked what doing business in Russia was really like, he simply said: "It's either passion or poison. There's nothing in between."

That first trip to Sochi—still a vast construction site at the time—was passion. A decade later, with bridges burned and trust dissolved, there is indeed nothing left in between.

Steven Parker is a payments and financial services professional who has lived and worked around the world. He studied Russian in school and first traveled to Moscow in 2006. From 2010 to 2013, he served as general manager for the Central and Eastern Europe region at a major international payments provider. He remains connected to the region through commercial and charitable work.

A PARTNER AND A CAT
Ivan Scalfarotto

I arrived in Moscow at the end of 2005, when it was still possible to believe that Russia wanted to open up to the world. I flew in from London, carrying a prestigious new job, an inadequate coat, and a healthy dose of youthful optimism. During my interview, I had asked the CEO, quite directly, whether my sexual orientation might be a problem. "Our colleagues are young, they speak English, they're cosmopolitan," he told me. "I really don't think it will be an issue."

So I accepted. And it worked. Moscow struck me as vibrant and dazzling, a mix between Paris and Tokyo, with grand boulevards, apocalyptic traffic, and a kind of austere beauty that took my breath away. I worked in banking, heading human resources not only in Russia but also in Ukraine and Kazakhstan. Russians, fortunately, are hierarchical by nature—and at the top of the pyramid, I might just be allowed not to conform.

But I quickly realized I wasn't in London anymore when I was asked to introduce myself for the company's internal newsletter. One of the questions was "Can you tell us about your family?" I replied, simply, "I'm here with my partner and my cat." A few days later, my deputy walked into my office, looking uneasy.

"They say one of your answers doesn't translate well into Russian: 'партнёр' just doesn't sound right. They're asking if you can change it to 'I am not married and I have a cat.'"

I smiled. "I don't want to say what I'm not. I want to say what I am."

So the interview was published as it was, on the front page. A few hours later, I received an internal email from a colleague: "I'm glad to have a brave person as my HR head. P.S. Please don't tell anyone I wrote to you."

That was when I understood that something beneath the bright surface was off. Still, you could breathe, speak, even hope. And for the entire time I lived there, I never stopped being myself. Today, that same phrase—"I have a partner and a cat"—probably wouldn't make it past spellcheck. And I, quite simply, couldn't go back to Moscow now. I wouldn't want to.

That interview—small, dusty, printed in two columns—remains, for me, a symbol of a vanished era. A time when, even in Russia, telling the truth was still possible.

Senator Ivan Scalfarotto is an Italian politician who has held several high-level government positions. He brings significant international experience from his earlier career in the financial sector. A longtime advocate for civil rights and democratic values, he combines public service with a global perspective.

Fidel the cat.

CONCRETE DREAM
Ambassador (Ret.) Michael Klecheski

For many of us who served at the U.S. Embassy in Moscow, the city's architecture was a source of fascination. The ponderous Stalinist wedding-cake–like structures known as the "Seven Sisters" were architectural notables. Just as compelling were their philosophical opposites: the early Soviet Constructivist buildings, stark and ambitious remnants of a brief, heady era of cultural and architectural experimentation.

Of these, the most mysterious was the Narkomfin, pressed against the rear of our modern embassy compound. Stained and crumbling, it loomed beyond a drab concrete wall. To us, it was just an eyesore. But once, it had been a dream in concrete. We despised it, seeing not a monument to idealism but a perch for Russia's secret police—watching and listening to us.

When our son, then studying architecture in the United States, visited Moscow, Russian architects we knew arranged for our family to visit the Narkomfin. Up close, the building's decay was even more apparent. Its crumbling front belied the excitement it must have stirred when it opened in 1932. Avant-garde architect Moisei Ginzburg had designed it with an attractive entrance through a park that, those many decades later, was strewn with garbage. Aiming to construct a space aligned with socialist ideology, he built apartments that lacked their own kitchens; residents were to meet—and presumably develop a collectivist spirit—in communal kitchens.

But as we stepped through its hollowed corridors, that vision lay in ruins. A handful of inhabited apartments had been reduced to squalid improvisations—hot plates perched on battered tables, tangled electrical wires dangling like veins exposed to the air. Most of the building was sealed off. We imagined the ever-watchful FSB stationed in the shadows, surveilling the embassy through peeling curtains and broken panes.

And yet, improbably, the building was not entirely empty of life. A young artist—a self-styled hippie—and his girlfriend welcomed us into their spartan living arrangement. For them, inhabiting this experiment in utopian living was worth the discomfort. They told us that things weren't terribly comfortable but that living in what had once been a symbol of cultural experimentation was worth the sacrifice.

Well, maybe. The Narkomfin—once a bold vision cast in concrete—had, over time, faded toward ruin, its watchtowers and whispers lingering as uneasy remnants of a utopian dream: fragile and unfinished.

Michael Klecheski served for more than thirty-five years in the U.S. Foreign Service, retiring after his assignment as ambassador to Mongolia from 2019 to 2022. He held multiple assignments in Russia and the Soviet Union, most recently from 2010 to 2013.

Editor's note: The Narkomfin's renovation, completed in 2020, restored its architectural integrity while adapting it for modern use, earning widespread praise for its sensitive, historically informed approach.

NO HAPPY ENDING
Edward Verona

As someone who lived in Russia during that hopeful first decade after the Soviet Union's collapse, I cannot look back without reflecting on the grim transformation since Vladimir Putin's rise. The dreams of joining the community of free and prosperous nations have long since withered under the relentless tightening of authoritarian rule. Democracy, human rights, and freedom of expression—once fragile but real—have been systematically dismantled.

There was a time when political debate echoed in the State Duma, when newspapers and television dared to broadcast opposing views, and ordinary citizens could speak without fear. Yes, the 1990s were chaotic—rife with corruption, scandal, and the bloody war in Chechnya. The path from the wreckage of central planning to a free market was steep, hindered further by collapsing oil prices. Yet by the decade's end, Russia was unmistakably moving toward a market economy and a freer society.

The 1998 ruble collapse was a brutal blow, but not a death knell. Economic reforms pushed forward, luring foreign investment and driving domestic growth. Rising oil and gas prices brought windfall revenues, and Russia's renegotiated debts and expanding markets earned it a place among the world's leading emerging economies.

For a time, even Putin's growing nationalism could be dismissed as posturing. Investors clung to hopes of deeper reforms, and the election of Dmitri Medvedev in 2008 offered a glimmer of possibility. His call for modernization—anchored in institutions, infrastructure, investment, and innovation—hinted at a Russia still eager to integrate with the global economy, still flirting with democratic ideals.

But illusions die hard. The 2008 invasion of Georgia could be rationalized as Putin's swan song. Washington's *reset* policy followed. Many of us, foolishly, still believed Russia could be a partner.

That hope dissolved swiftly. Flawed elections, Putin's return, and a chilling pattern of violence against political opponents—Boris Nemtsov, Alexei Navalny, and others—laid bare the regime's true nature. Support for Assad's brutal war in Syria, the annexation of Crimea, the bloodshed in Donbas, and the full-scale invasion of Ukraine erased any lingering doubt.

"Once upon a time in Russia" had all the makings of a fairy tale. But there will be no "happily ever after."

Edward S. Verona served as a U.S. diplomat and later as a business executive in Russia. He was president of the U.S.–Russia Business Council from 2008 to 2013.

BORN IN OCCUPATION, LIVING IN FREEDOM
Merle Pormeister

I was born in Soviet-occupied Estonia in 1967, during a time when the country had been forcibly annexed by the USSR. When I graduated from the University of Tartu in 1990—one of Europe's oldest universities—the occupation was finally coming to an end. As a student, I took part in Estonia's fight for freedom: the Singing Revolution, the mass gatherings, the refusal to remain silent.

From 1997 to 2020, I served as an Estonian diplomat, with postings in Greece, Moscow, St. Petersburg, and Kyiv. I witnessed the slow shifting of Eastern Europe's tectonic plates—often from the front row. In Kyiv (2014–18), I stood beside my Ukrainian friends in their struggle for sovereignty. In Moscow, I stood in something far colder.

I arrived at the Estonian embassy in Moscow in the summer of 2007, shortly after the Bronze Soldier crisis in Estonia. That spring, Estonia had relocated a Soviet war memorial from central Tallinn to a military cemetery. Russia responded with fury: violent protests, cyberattacks on our banks and institutions, and a smear campaign against our leadership. It was the world's first major cyberwar—and Estonia stood its ground.

By the time I arrived in Moscow, tensions were high. The Estonian embassy, located near Arbat Street, bore small bullet holes in its windows. Graffiti scrawled on nearby walls read "Death to Marina" (our ambassador) and "Death to Estonians." Protesters gathered daily. Inside, we tried to maintain diplomatic calm, but the atmosphere was heavy with threat.

On my first evening, I went to buy some groceries. I lost my bearings on the way back to the embassy. Afraid to admit I was Estonian, I asked strangers for directions to the Dutch embassy, which happened to be next door. In those days, I carried two truths: I was proudly Estonian—and I dared not say so aloud.

When strangers asked where I was from, I said Finland. Our languages are similar enough for the lie to pass. Still, it never felt right.

Looking back, I feel as though I have lived many lives. I spent my first twenty years, metaphorically speaking, in a Soviet prison, then helped sow the seeds of Estonian freedom. As a diplomat, I helped shape the country that grew from that soil—a digital democracy that joined NATO and the EU and stood tall in a dangerous region.

But we Estonians know how fragile freedom can be—and how close the shadows still are.

Merle Pormeister served as a consul of Estonia in Moscow for two-month assignments in the summer of 2007 and the winter of 2009, and in St. Petersburg during five separate postings between 2006 and 2013.

THE MURDER OF BORIS NEMTSOV
Ambassador (Ret.) John Tefft

At 1:30 a.m. on February 28, 2015, my wife, Mariella, woke me in the master bedroom of Spaso House, the American ambassador's residence in Moscow. She told me CNN was reporting the murder of Boris Nemtsov. He had been shot in the back two hours earlier on the Bolshoi Moskvoretsky Bridge, just below the Kremlin, while walking home from dinner with his partner, Anna Duritskaya. Groggy from a long week at work, I joined Mariella to watch the coverage, then emailed my staff to say we should discuss our response in the morning.

I couldn't shake the thought that Nemtsov's murder was part of a grim pattern. The human rights activist and politician Galina Starovoitova and journalist Anna Politkovskaya—talented leaders—were murdered in their prime. I had met both during my service as deputy chief of mission in Moscow in the late 1990s. Now Nemtsov, a charismatic politician with so much promise, was added to that tragic list. How could Russia ever thrive while losing its brightest minds to violence?

By morning, the internet was abuzz with news of hundreds of Russians gathering on the bridge, laying flowers in tribute. I decided to join them. I called my staff and asked them to meet me at the bridge. When we arrived, the bridge was packed with people. Many Russians recognized me and made way for our group. My deputy, Lynne Tracy, and others accompanied me as we laid bouquets at the growing shrine—a mountain of flowers, photos of Nemtsov, and flickering candles marking the spot where he had fallen. It was profoundly moving. Journalists and television crews captured the moment, and the footage quickly spread online. As we left, I told the press:

> *"All of us at the American embassy and the many American Foreign Service officers who knew Boris Nemtsov mourn his tragic death today. As governor of Nizhny Novgorod, deputy prime minister, and as a leader of the political opposition, Boris Nemtsov stood for the best in Russia and ably represented the Russian people.*

We join our president and secretary of state in calling on the Russian authorities to investigate this heinous murder expeditiously and bring to justice those responsible."

On Monday, I attended Nemtsov's memorial at the Sakharov Center, paying my respects to his grieving mother and children. I conveyed the condolences of President Obama and Secretary Kerry. All of us felt a profound sense of grief and loss—for Nemtsov, but also for Russia.

John Tefft served as the American ambassador to Russia from 2014 to 2017 and as deputy chief of mission from 1996 to 1999. He also served as the United States ambassador to Lithuania, Georgia, and Ukraine.

THE MEMORY THAT STAYED
John McNaughton

I've struggled to write about Russia—not for lack of stories, but because one memory eclipses the rest. Until I confront it, the lighter, more amusing moments others may recall so easily remain out of reach.

Since 1988, I've lived and worked across the Soviet Union and post-Soviet space. I love Russia—its people, its culture, its language. I have dear friends there. One of my children was born there. I still hope, perhaps impossibly, to return. But that hope is shadowed by sorrow.

When the war began, I was living in Prague and working for a Russian firm. The initial shock quickly gave way to a wave of Ukrainian refugees. Many came from the Donbas and spoke Russian—the language of Pushkin, of lullabies—and now, for many, the language of loss.

The Czech people responded with admirable compassion. Among my Russian friends, disbelief prevailed. They couldn't accept what their country was doing. My Ukrainian friends, meanwhile, were frozen by fear.

I remember meeting Igor, a Ukrainian colleague, for coffee. He looked hollowed out. When I asked why, he showed me a photo of his brother—a young man in a muddy field, holding a shovel.

"He's digging a trench," Igor said. "That's where he'll be living. They call it 'digging our own graves.'"

That image—of a man forced to carve a hole in the earth and live in it—haunted me. But something a child said lingered even more.

One afternoon, while playing mini-golf with my son, a little girl approached us and spoke in Russian. "Hi, I'm Maria. I speak three languages—Russian, Ukrainian, and Czech."

Then she added, with solemn pride, "My father couldn't come with us. Someone had to stay home and take care of our cat."

That simple sentence shattered me. The cruelty of war isn't abstract. It's a child in exile trying to explain her father's absence with a story that's easier to bear.

War defies expression because it's made up of countless private heartbreaks—each distinct, each unbearable. A little girl who may never see her father again. A father who may be gone, or who lives each day apart from his children. I know there are stories more harrowing than this. But this is the one that has never left me.

Russia gave me so much. But now, it also gives me grief. And that grief clouds even the brightest memories.

John McKnaughton has traveled and worked in the former Communist bloc since 1988 in various spheres of finance and commerce.

ACKNOWLEDGMENTS

This book exists only because of the generous and thoughtful contributions of more than one hundred individuals whose stories, memories, and reflections fill its pages. Each account is distinct, yet together they form a collective portrait that captures something of the spirit, contradictions, and enduring mystery of a Russia that once was. Thank you for giving your time, your insights, and—above all—your honesty.

I owe particular thanks to Bernie Sucher, a colleague from my Moscow days, whose long-overdue reunion with me in a Chicago speakeasy in 2024 unfolded into hours of nostalgic storytelling, half-forgotten names, and generous pours. Somewhere between the second cocktail and the third anecdote, the idea for this anthology was born.

I am equally indebted to Guy Archer, my friend and former colleague at the American Chamber of Commerce in Moscow. In every stage of the project, he offered invaluable guidance on its structure, and through his generous network many contributors found their way into these pages. His steady encouragement and unwavering belief in the work helped carry it forward.

I also want to thank Svetlana Rukhelman and Cris Martin of the Davis Center at Harvard University, who engaged with the project from its outset. Their early interest and encouragement helped strengthen the foundation on which this anthology was built.

I am further grateful to Rachel and Marc Polonsky, Eric Rubin, and Daniel Satinsky, whose parallel effort—The Satinsky Archive (https://therussiaprogram.org/satinsky_archive) which preserves oral histories of the era—played an important role in shaping this project's reach. Through their generous advice and introductions, I was connected with experts in the Russia field who offered endorsements, insights, and support.

Beyond those I can name here, I am deeply grateful to the many friends and associates whose quiet efforts broadened the circle of this project, encouraging participation, connecting me with new contributors, and ensuring that memories that might otherwise have been lost found their place in these pages.

To all who lent their voices, their lenses, or simply their time—thank you for helping preserve a shared memory of a vanished era.

Steven A. Fisher
Chicago, Illinois
September 2025

PHOTO CREDITS

Photographs accompanying individual essays were provided by the contributors unless otherwise noted below.

The following photographs are in the public domain or released under a Creative Commons license and are attributed as follows:

Dabbar, p. 25. "Oil Terminal." *Oil & Gas Journal*. (www.ogj.com)
Lee, p. 35. "FX." *The Moscow Times*. (https://www.themoscowtimes.com/2014/11/06/ruble-rout-accelerates-as-russias-central-bank-stands-aside-a41086)
Tay, p. 37. "Meeting with Martynov." (https://thefoundation.sg/news-building-bridges-music-sgn/)
Kuchins, p. 39. "Moscow Business District." Dmitry A. Mottl, own work. CC BY-SA 3.0. (https://commons.wikimedia.org/w/index.php?curid=4461552)
Zimbler, p. 49. "Moscow Metro." Bernt Rostad, Kitai-Gorod Station, 2008. CC BY 2.0.
Gruger, p. 51. "Moscow Traffic." TheCollector.com.
Pugh, p. 55. "Horses." Margarita Gromova, Pexels.com.
Archer, p. 71. "Burnt Pages." Freepik.com.
Katta, p. 75. "Snowprints." Andrei!Flickr/CC.
Mankoff, p. 81. "Altai Village." HappyFrogTravels.com.
Grisel, p. 83. "Road." (https://pixabay.com/photos/road-horizon-lonely-alone-7726202/)
Pomeranz, p. 85. "Civil Code." Yandex Market.ru.
Firestone, J., p. 87. "Steering Wheel." Steven Fisher.
Sucher, p. 93. "Basketball Sorrow." *The New York Times*. (https://www.nytimes.com/2022/09/09/sports/olympics/usa-soviet-union-olympics-basketball.html)
FitzGerald, p. 95. "Courtyard." Photographer unknown, public domain.
Jenkins, p. 97. "Airport Seats." (https://www.vagabondjourney.com/moscow-sheremetyavo-the-worlds-scariest-airport/)

Costello, p. 99. "Disco Party." Alexander Uchkin/TASS.
Klecheski, E., p. 109. "Rocking Horse." Markellos, Wikipedia.com.
Courtney, p. 115. "Wounded." TASS.
Aris, p. 117. "Soldier." Voki Rulovic, on X. (https://x.com/VokiRulovic/status/1947653698139623703)
Conn, p. 121. "Turkey." StockCake.com.
Shor, p. 123. "Zyuganov." (https://et.m.wikipedia.org/wiki/Fail:Gennady_Zyuganov,_2013.jpeg)
Menu, p. 129. "Airport Hall." Photographer unknown, public domain.
Belin, p. 133. "Central Bank." Ludvig14, CC BY-SA 4.0. (https://creativecommons.org/licenses/by-sa/4.0, via Wikimedia Commons)
Ridlington, p. 135. "Golf Ball." Kindel Media, Pexels.com.
Thunem, p. 151. "Traffic Police." *The Moscow Times*. (https://www.themoscowtimes.com/2015/11/12/russian-traffic-police-to-go-undercover-a50748)
Creitzman, p. 159. "Black Snow." *The Siberian Times*.
Borden, p. 161. "Crowd." Rakoon. Creative Commons CC0 1.0 Universal Public Domain Dedication. (https://commons.wikimedia.org/wiki/File:0023_August_14th_2016_in_Moscow.jpg)
Giaquinto, p. 163. "Snow-Bound Cars." Elena Naletova, Depositphotos.com
Melling, p. 165. "Broken Teacup." Kintsugilabo.com.
Luhmann, p. 173. "Halloween." Jonathan Cooper, Pexels.com.
Tulgan, p. 175. "Cheese." Photographer unknown, public domain.
Mahan, p. 177. "Tupolev Interior." Christo. (https://commons.wikimedia.org/wiki/File:Budapest,_Aeropark_Múzeum,_Tupolev-154_B-2_(HA-LCG),_11.jpg)
Firestone, T., p. 179. "Toilet in Repair." (https://tvin270584.livejournal.com/1404976.html)
Ostling, p. 183. "Nightclub." Maor Attias, Pexels.com.
Stobie, p. 185. "Saratov Vodka." Minibottlelibrary.com.
Salonen, p. 193. "Okudzhava Monument." (https://russianlandmarks.wordpress.com/wp-content/uploads/2014/11/img_90452.jpg)
Knaus, p. 197. "Vodka and Pickle." Serge Che, Flickr.com.
Roazen, p. 207. "Kindergarten." TeachinRussia.com.

Dauman, p. 219. "Warehouse." Peter H., Pixabay.com.

Power, p. 221. "Woman Holding Pistol." Tima Miroshnichenko, Pexels.com.

Parker, p. 223. "Banya." WanderlustingK.com. (https://www.wanderlustingk.com/travel-blog/russian-banya)

Klecheski, M., p. 227. "Narkomfin Ruins." Archi.ru. Photo courtesy of Ginsburg Architects.

Verona, p. 229. "OMON." Sergey Rodovnichenko, via Wikimedia Commons. CC BY-SA 2.0. AFPGA.

Tefft, p. 233. "Nemtsov." (https://commons.m.wikimedia.org/wiki/File:There_are_flowers_and_candles_near_the_site_of_the_murder_of_Boris_Nemtsov_cropped.jpg)

McNaughton, p. 235. "Girl on Train." vecteezy_prague-czech-republic-october-5-2023-little-girl_41152349.mov.

The following photograph is reproduced with permission:

Fraissinet, p. 47. "Moscow night" by Marie de La Ville Baugé.

I am grateful to the photographers and institutions who have made their images available for use in this volume. Every effort has been made to provide accurate credit and sourcing information. If you believe any photo attribution is in error, please contact me so that future editions may be corrected.

ABOUT THE EDITOR

Steven A. Fisher is a finance professional and independent scholar whose thirty-five years with Citibank took him across emerging markets, including sixteen in senior leadership roles in Moscow and Kyiv. He has spoken at finance and policy forums worldwide, offering insights shaped by decades on the ground.

His works include *Failure. Russia Under Putin*, coedited with Harley D. Balzer (Brookings Institution Press, 2025), and *Into Russia's Cauldron: An American Vision, Undone* (Forest Cat Press, 2021). He is also the coauthor, with Anders Åslund, of *New Challenges and Dwindling Returns for Russia's National Champions* (Atlantic Council, 2020).

A graduate of Georgetown University's School of Foreign Service (M.S.) and Cornell University (B.A. in Sino-Soviet studies), he speaks fluent Russian.

www.ingramcontent.com/pod-product-compliance
Lightning Source LLC
Chambersburg PA
CBHW071958070526
44583CB00015B/1241